➤ I am not satisfied with the repair on my car. Do I give the mechanic a second chance—and should I be expected to pay?

➤ Should I use the dealership where I bought my car as my mechanic?

➤ After I paid for my repair and drove away, I noticed I still had the problem. How do I know the repair I asked for was really ever done? Should I demand a test drive before I pay for a repair?

➤ If I leave my car keys with a mechanic or a tow truck, how can I avoid the risk of having my car keys duplicated?

➤ I suspect a mechanic used recycled oil and antifreeze and sold it to me as premium grade. Can I prove it?

➤ Is it a good idea to make friends with my repair shop manager or is it better to keep it strictly business?

➤ I know nothing about cars except how to turn the key. How can I be of help to my mechanic in pinpointing a problem with my car?

➤ I think I smell gasoline. Is my car safe to drive or should I get my car towed to a repair shop?

WHAT THE "EXPERTS" MAY *NOT* TELL YOU ABOUT™ . . . CAR REPAIR COULD LEAVE YOU STRANDED!

In this hands-on guide, you'll learn to navigate the road map of car repair and maintenance, get good value for your money, and never get shafted again!

WHAT THE "EXPERTS" MAY *NOT* TELL YOU ABOUT™ ...

Car Repair

MITCHELL ZELMAN

WARNER BOOKS

NEW YORK   BOSTON

Some entries in "Glossary of Terms" were excerpted with permission from *Motor Age Automotive Glossary* 2002. *Motor Age* is a copyrighted publication of Advanstar Communications Inc. All rights reserved.

Warner Books

Time Warner Book Group
1271 Avenue of the Americas, New York, NY 10020
Visit our Web site at www.twbookmark.com.

Printed in the United States of America

First Printing: July 2004
10 9 8 7 6 5 4 3 2 1

Library of Congress Cataloging-in-Publication Data
Zelman, Mitchell.
      What the "experts" may not tell you about car repair / Mitchell Zelman.
          p.   cm.
      Includes index.
      ISBN 0-446-69094-5
    1. Automobiles—Maintenance and repair—Popular works.   I. Title.
      TL152.Z43   2004
      629.28'72—dc22   2004003581

Book design and text composition by Stratford Publishing Services

Cover photo courtesy of Mitchell Zelman

To my parents, who taught me that the best job in the world is the one that you enjoy going to.

To Sara, Ryan, Brandon, and Melissa for making my life . . . so interesting

Acknowledgments

I would like to acknowledge and thank the following people for sharing their insight in their areas of expertise:

Alan Jabr for his expertise on tires.

Eduard Lebedev for his input on trouble codes (and check engine lights).

James McGrory, ASE Master Technician since 1977, for critiquing the technical correctness of this book.

John Randazzo for painting a clear picture on body and fender repair.

Brian Stein for sharing years of experience on exhaust systems with me.

Shy Yair for his expertise on air-conditioning, glass, and lock repair.

Contents

A Note from the Author

*T*he purpose of this book is twofold: first, to make you a more responsible and aware car owner who needs to make fewer trips to the mechanic; and second, to protect you from unscrupulous mechanics by informing you of the normal practices of honest mechanics and the common scams the dishonest ones employ. It explains in the most simplified terms the mechanical function of serviceable parts that are commonly replaced and maintained in your vehicle. Having a better understanding of the way your car functions not only prevents unnecessary trips to the mechanic, it also enables you to feel confident that you are not getting ripped off when you do take your car in.

What the "Experts" May Not Tell You will teach you how to find and do business with a good mechanic and will also advise you about the scams and techniques that repair facilities use in their deception. After reading this book you will know how to "talk the talk and walk the walk" in your repair shop. A mechanic will think twice before trying to pull the wool over your eyes.

PART 1

Learning About Your Car

What Destroys Cars?

If you were to put your new car on a lift, start it, and put it into drive, with the exception of changing the oil and filter and adding fuel, it would probably run for well over 100,000 miles without a hitch. From that point, with the proper preventative maintenance, it could do it again. But that same new car on the road encounters many adverse obstacles and stresses.

Road conditions. The ideal road is one that is open, flat, straight, and smooth. The worst is one that is bumpy and congested with many sharp turns. "Stop and go" traffic situations put strain on the engine, drivetrain, brakes, and suspension.

Climate. The ideal climate for cars is one that does not get excessively hot or excessively cold. Extreme heat causes parts to expand, crack, or melt. Extreme cold causes parts to contract and become brittle and stiff. A vehicle kept in a heated garage will outlast a vehicle parked under a foot of snow.

Driving styles. Ideally, if you baby your car it will outlast one that is pushed to its limits. Your car was built to be driven, so drive it, but do not punch it out, push it through hard turns, jam on the brakes to stop, and then expect it to last forever. A car purchased from the little old lady from Pasadena will surely be in better shape than a car purchased from Speed Racer.

Functionality. Compare a three-year-old car driven by a salesman on long trips to the same three-year-old car driven for a car service. There is no comparison. The salesman's car will be in much better shape across the board.

Environment. Do you live near the coast? Salty air penetrates into every space of your vehicle and in due time will corrode exposed surfaces. Salt that is spread on the roadways during the winter will eat away at exposed surfaces and imbed in nooks and crannies, where it will become like a cancerous tumor.

Lifestyles. If you are always in a rush, chances are you will not warm up your car on a cold day, you will accelerate harder to get where you are going, and you will brake harder to stop when you get there—not to mention the risk of crashing.

Over-revving. Driving at high speeds, shifting at the red line (manual transmissions), or forcing your car out of a snowbound parking spot puts added stress on your engine and transmission. Take it down a notch . . .

Poor maintenance. Ignoring the maintenance requirements of your vehicle will eventually take its toll and can affect other parts of the car. Ignoring sounds and odors can be a big mistake, as these can be signs of a serious problem.

Faulty repairs. Every time you have a repair performed on your car it is with the intention of correcting or avoiding a mechanical problem. If the repair is not done properly, your vehicle's integrity is compromised. If the repair was made on your power sunroof, well, maybe you will get rained on if it will not close. But if the shabby repair was made on your brake hose, that could be another story . . .

Kids. Food, drinks, cigarettes, sharp objects, using the passenger compartment to carry things other than passengers—all can lead to the destruction of your beautiful car.

Exterior aesthetics. Protecting your vehicle's finish from the elements by washing and waxing it periodically will help it last much longer.

Remember that two identical cars that roll off the assembly line one after the other could be found years later, one in great shape while the other is ready for the scrap heap. It was not that the cars were built any differently from each other. It was because of the care and maintenance—or lack thereof—that the vehicles' owners gave to their cars over the years.

Service Contracts

Nowadays, new cars are being built better than ever. They require less and less maintenance because of new technology. As a result, new car manufacturers offer long warranty periods. However, because of the points listed above (and more!), all vehicles will eventually require maintenance and repair. How well your car was maintained and where and how hard it was driven will determine how it will fare when it gets on in years.

If you are the original owner of your vehicle and you have maintained it fairly well from the get-go, you should not expect any major breakdowns for the first 50,000 miles or so. At this juncture in your vehicle's life, you should consider a few points. If you can afford to purchase a new car every three to four years then you may want to start shopping. If you cannot afford to, and you want to see your car last for many years without pouring good money into it, consider a service contract (extended warranty) to protect you from the high costs of repairing your vehicle.

Insurance companies offer plans that will cover the expense of repairing your vehicle should it need repair. There are a wide range of plans that cover anything from a faulty cigarette lighter to rebuilding your engine or transmission. Choose a plan that pays for "new," not used, replacement parts. Before deciding on a particular plan be sure to read the fine print and understand what will not be covered. Look for a plan that offers a zero deductible even if you have to pay a few hundred dollars more for the policy. This will save you money in the long run. If you select a plan with a deductible, find out the terms of the deductible. Under some service contracts you pay one charge (deductible) per visit for repairs, no matter how many. Other contracts require a deductible payment for *each* unrelated repair. For example, your vehicle develops a leak from the water pump, which is a component covered by your extended insurance plan. You bring your vehicle into the shop to have it repaired and while it is being repaired the mechanic notices that your shock absorber (another covered part) is leaking. Will your insurance company apply the deductible only once or will they consider the repairs as two separate incidents as these components are not related, and apply the deductible twice? For more facts on service contracts go to the Federal Trade Commission for the Consumer Web site at www.ftc.gov/bcp/conline/pubs/autos/autoserv.htm. Also, you can contact the Better Business Bureau or your state insurance commission to see if there have been any complaints against a specific insurance company.

Also look for a plan that will cover overheating and related problems. *Note:* Salvage titles will void this warranty. Salvage titles are titles given to cars that were considered total losses by the insurance companies due to fire, vandalism, collision, theft, or flood. These cars are purchased and repaired by body shops. They then have to pass a strict inspection to determine if they are safe before they can be re-registered. The new title will then say "salvage" on it.

Additional benefits of these plans might include towing, car rental, tire coverage, road service, and trip interruption, which would pay for lodging and meals while your car is being repaired. For those who lease vehicles, some plans include turn-in protection, which will cover against any body damage the vehicle has when you return it at the end of your lease.

Different plans are available for cars with both low mileage or high mileage, but the least expensive plans are offered to vehicles that are still covered by the manufacturer's warranty.

Insurance companies are in business to make money. They do this by taking in more money than they shell out. Hopefully your vehicle will not suck you dry, but if you feel that it is on the verge of doing that you should consider this coverage. There is a Web site called "Extended Warranty Buyer's Guide" (www.extended-warranty.info) that can help you decide on the right policy for you and your car.

Maintenance

New vehicles, barring any manufacturing or engineering defects, require very little maintenance for the first 15,000–20,000 miles. You should familiarize yourself with your vehicle by reading your owner's manual and maintenance schedule, which should serve as your guide. Changing the engine oil and oil filter every 3,000 miles, rotating the tires every 6,000–9,000 miles, and maintaining the proper tire pressure is generally all that is needed for new vehicles.

Insider's Tip

New car dealers offer scheduled maintenance at high prices. If your car has less than 20,000 miles you should not and will not need much. Many of the items on their checklist can be checked by a qualified mechanic during a routine oil and filter change.

Used or older cars require a little more attention. By 20,000 miles, depending on driving conditions, brake pads could wear down due to the friction exerted against them each time you brake. Some cars have brake sensors that will activate a warning light on the dashboard when the brake pads wear thin. Others have metal squeak indicators that will squeak when your pads are worn out.

Fluid levels are another concern. Check the levels of the following fluids: oil, transmission, power steering, brake, antifreeze, and windshield washer. Check the wiper blades for cracks or streaking. Clean them with a paper towel and Windex before you decide to replace them. Clean the windshield. If you do a lot of stop-and-go driving, have the motor and transmission mounts checked at this time.

Many people do not replace their belts or hoses until they fail, and eventually they all will fail. A recent national voluntary vehicle inspection program by the Car Care Council (www.carcare.org) found that 24 percent of belts and 19 percent of hoses checked were in need of replacement. And there is no good time to be stranded. In addition, your engine will overheat from a broken belt or hose. This can cause serious and expensive damage.

What causes belts to break? Heat, age, and high mileage are the culprits. The engine compartment is very hot and the bending of the belts as they go around the pulleys creates more heat.

Serpentine belts are more commonly used on today's engines, spinning the power steering pulley, air-conditioning compressor, alternator, and water pump. If this one belt breaks, all of the above will stop working and the vehicle will be dead in the water. Serpentine belts should be replaced every four to five years or 50,000–60,000 miles. V-belts should be replaced every three to four years or 40,000–50,000 miles. Timing belts should be replaced every 60,000 miles, although some newer models boast timing belts that last 100,000 miles.

Hoses carry antifreeze through the cooling system. They are subjected to extreme heat and cold. After enough time hoses can become hard and brittle. In many cases they balloon and burst.

The problem for many mechanics is that a hose may look fine from the outside but it might be deteriorating from the inside. This is why it is a good idea to replace all the hoses every four years or 48,000 miles as a measure of preventative maintenance. Care should be taken by the mechanic not to damage the neck of the radiator or heater core while removing the old hose. New clamps should be used to ensure a tight squeeze.

If you drive over bumpy conditions, have the suspension checked. This would include the steering linkage, ball joints, struts or shocks, control arm bushings, and sway bar links.

Aside from your routine oil and filter change, you might be in need of a new air filter and fuel filter. The air filter prevents small particles such as dust and sand from entering the air intake manifold. Traveling on dirt roads and driveways will cause this filter to clog faster, preventing the free flow of air into the engine. This can cause poor engine performance resulting in sluggish acceleration and decreased fuel mileage. Some newer vehicles come equipped with "cabin" filters. These prevent dirty air from being blown into the interior compartment through the heater or A/C vents. If they are clogged you can blow air pressure through them to clean them, or purchase new ones.

The fuel filter prevents dirty fuel from entering the fuel intake system. Dirty fuel can result from a dirty or rusty gas tank, or possibly from sediment floating around in the gas station tank when you are filling up. Dirt in your fuel will clog your fuel filter, causing poor performance, and if completely clogged will cause your engine to stop running. A third source of dirty fuel could come from vandalism. You should always lock your gas cap.

Gasoline goes stale after five or six months. If you know you will not be using your vehicle for an extended period of time, a fuel preservative or stabilizer should be added. Follow the product's instructions.

Warming Up Your Engine

Even though many mechanics or manufacturers may tell you that it is not necessary to warm up your engine, I can tell you from my years of experience that it is very important to do so, especially on cold days. When it is cold out, your engine oil becomes thick and sits in the base of your oil pan. When you first start your engine, the moving parts have no oil pressure to protect them from the tremendous amount of friction. This is called a dry start. As the engine runs, the oil thins and lubricates. The metal parts of your engine expand from the heat and fit tighter and better in relation to one another. Usually hydraulic ticking subsides and the engine runs smoothly. To take a cold engine and throw it into gear and ask it to move the weight of your vehicle is asking a lot. Your engine is not a light bulb. It may be on when you start it on a cold day, but it is not ready. On days when the temperature is above 50 degrees Fahrenheit, I would recommend warming up your engine for thirty seconds, and on days when the temperature is between 30 and 50 degrees I recommend one full minute. On days below 30 degrees, a minimum of two minutes is necessary.

General Precautions

Before we go into the things that could go wrong with your car, here is a list of sensible rules to be followed when you start tinkering around.

Exercise extreme caution when refueling. Static electricity can ignite fuel vapors when you are refueling. Always touch the side of the car, not near the filler, or touch the metal near the pump away from any source of gas before touching the gas pump nozzle.

Never put yourself or any body parts under a car when lifting it or when it is jacked up. Never jack a car up on anything but level ground with the parking brake on.

Never use a droplight in the presence of fuel. A droplight is a potential igniter of fuel.

Out of respect for heat, moving parts, and high voltage, never touch anything in the engine compartment when the car is running.

Never wear a tie, braids, or jewelry of any kind that could be drawn into the engine's fan, belts, or other moving parts.

Never put your face directly over the carburetor or battery.

Never touch high-voltage ignition wires when the car is running.

Never touch the fan blades, even when the engine is off.

Never open up a radiator cap when the engine is hot.

Be aware of remote starter switches when you work on your car.

Never stand in water with a droplight or other electrical device.

Never run your engine indoors.

Never work on your car with children in or around it.

Always wear gloves and eye protection when handling a car battery.

Always use your head. Think it through.

Protect the environment. Dispose of oil, antifreeze, batteries, and tires properly.

PART 2

How Things Work

*T*he following sections, arranged in alphabetical order, contain important information that will help you understand the mechanics of the different systems of your vehicle. Having a basic understanding of how something works can make the difference between being robbed blind or being given a fair deal. Service manuals are available for purchase for most model cars, and it would be advisable to read specific information about a specific repair before you bring your car into the shop. This will enable you to have an informed conversation with the technician.

Air-Conditioning: How to Take the Chill out of Air-Conditioning Repair

It is another hot day and you turn on your air conditioner, and hot air blows out of the vents. "What's wrong?" you ask yourself. Well, the possibilities range from a simple fix like a fuse to a serious and expensive repair like a bad evaporator (evaporator leaks are sometimes accompanied by an unusual odor inside the vehicle). Teaching you to be an air-conditioning technician is not the point behind this book; however, I can enlighten you on some steps that should be taken to get to the source of the problem.

It is crucial to understand that the air-conditioning system is sensitive to many factors that affect its performance. That is because, unlike a very straightforward, obvious repair on your vehicle, the air-conditioning system has components that cannot be determined to be working until the system is ready to be tested. Replacing a damaged compressor may be step one, adding the refrigerant may be step two. But only after the refrigerant is added might the technician discover that the expansion valve is clogged. The point is, you may be led down the path of multiple air-conditioning-related problems as they present themselves and find that you are spending hundreds of dollars with each repair, sometimes resulting in a functioning system and sometimes not. It would be risky for a technician to guarantee that the system will work perfectly after he changes one part, as there are many parts that could be faulty. He should guarantee only the work and the part that he did replace or repair.

If your A/C is blowing cooler air than the ambient outside temperature, but not cold air, then chances are the fuse is not blown. The compressor, which compresses and transfers refrigerant through the system, is working, and the system may just need to be recharged with refrigerant. Pre-1995 cars used the refrigerant R12, which depletes the earth's ozone layer. Currently R134a, an environmentally accepted gas, is being used. A technician should check the operating pressure of the system to determine if it is low.

If the A/C is blowing warm air when on the coldest A/C setting, then one of the possibilities is that all the refrigerant in the system has escaped. In any case, when refrigerant has escaped, the leak must be located and repaired to prevent the future escape of the gas. Leaks from the A/C system can be located by a few different means. The most basic way is to visually inspect all the different components, specifically where they connect to a hose or fitting, and look for any wetness around these connections. Oil is mixed with the refrigerant to lubricate the compressor. The leaking refrigerant and oil will leave a wet stain that usually attracts dirt. For instance, if you find a wet and dirty stain on a high-pressure hose, especially next to a connecting point, it's likely you have located your leak. Another way a technician would determine if there was still a leak would be by evacuating the system. This is done by sucking any and all air or refrigerant out of the lines with a vacuum pump, thereby creating a vacuum. Once the proper vacuum is reached on his vacuum gauge (minus 25–minus 30 lbs.) it is carefully monitored. If the gauge holds the vacuum for a specified period of time (15–20 minutes) the technician knows there are no more leaks. (Some shops prefer to hold the car overnight for checking small leaks.) If it fails to hold the vacuum, he knows there is a leak and can determine by the vacuum loss if the leak is small or large.

The next step to find a leak would be to add refrigerant with a dye additive. This leaves a stain visible with the aid of an ultraviolet light. The stain will reveal any and all leaks. Minor leaks will show traces of dye after two to three hours of continuous usage.

Aside from leaks, a common cause of A/C failure is a bad compressor. The compressor, which is spun via the air-conditioning belt or serpentine belt (both should be checked periodically to ensure that they are tight and in good condition), compresses the refrigerant and forces it through the system.

If the compressor goes bad it is usually accompanied by a knocking noise. Sometimes the compressor seizes altogether, causing the A/C belt to screech or break. It is important to realize that if your A/C compressor belt breaks and it also controls the water pump, your engine will quickly overheat.

Other kinds of collateral damage can result from a bad compressor. Small particles can break off inside the compressor and then travel and clog other parts in the system, such as the expansion valve, leading to further problems.

A partially blocked orifice tube will prevent your A/C from performing efficiently. Ice, sludge, or debris can form on the orifice tube. This excessive moisture and debris should be vacuum-purged overnight to clean out the system.

Most A/C systems have a built-in sight glass, which is a small see-through glass about a quarter of an inch in diameter. It is used to look for the presence of bubbles while the A/C is working. Bubbles in the sight glass would be an indicator that the system needs to be recharged with refrigerant. Systems that use R134a do not have a sight glass, as the oil in this refrigerant

Insider's Tip

If the system is blowing cool but not cold, check and clean, if necessary, the condenser, which is located in front of the radiator. Bugs and leaves can clog and block the passage of cool air, compromising the system's ability to produce cold air. Check in between the condenser and the radiator, as this is where debris can lodge. Also check the vents just in front of the windshield. These are the air intake vents for the heater and A/C, and leaves or snow can block them, reducing the air flow. Some cars have cabin filters located here that need to be serviced or replaced periodically.

causes a cloudiness that might be mistaken for bubbles, and a technician might then overcharge the system, damaging it.

Keep in mind that water dripping from the bottom of your vehicle when the A/C is working on hot days is just normal condensation running off the evaporator.

Insider's Tip

Your A/C system has a low-pressure and a high-pressure safety switch. If either of these switches becomes disconnected from its wire harness, the compressor will not function. The switches may have been disconnected during a previous repair and overlooked. Check or have these connections checked before you spend money on repairs.

In general, moisture is your A/C system's enemy number one. If your system has been opened (because of a broken hose or a part temporarily removed) for even a few days, moisture that is present in the air will get in and mix with the refrigerant, forming a corrosive acid. If this is the case, you should replace your receiver-drier (which removes moisture) and evacuate the system before recharging.

Insider's Tip

Nasty odors emanating from your car, especially when its A/C is on, could be either from a fungus growing on the evaporator or possibly from a dead rodent that was trapped in there. Have the evaporator cleaned and sanitized with a fungicide to kill any microbes. Have the drainage tubes cleaned to keep the condensation draining away from the evaporator.

Axles and Constant Velocity (CV) Joints

The front wheels receive their turning power through the axles. On front-wheel-drive cars, the axles not only have to spin as they propel the front wheels, they also have to pivot as the car goes over bumps and as the wheels change direction through turns. This pivoting would not be possible if the axle was a solid, rigid bar. CV joints, or constant velocity joints, are constructed into the axle assembly. These CV joints are surrounded by rubber boots shaped like accordions, which keep the necessary lubricating grease packed into the joint itself. If the accordion boot cracks, the grease spins out of the crack due to centrifical force, causing the CV joint to become unlubricated and eventually to fail. The boot is usually the first part of the axle to fail. It cracks due to age, extreme temperature, and excessive pivoting.

How would you know if you needed an axle replaced?

First, locate the axles by looking behind the wheels. Inspect the rubber accordion-shaped boots for cracks. If a crack is present, it would be accompanied by grease in and around the axle area, including on other parts sprayed by the spin-off of grease.

Another indication of a bad CV joint would be a *click-click-click* noise from the front of the car when you make a sharp turn or U-turn.

What should be considered to remedy this problem?

If the CV joint makes noise or vibrates, replace the entire axle with a rebuilt one, which comes complete with new CV joints and boots. If just the boot is cracked, you can opt to replace the boot alone, which is the less expensive way out. Considering that there is some labor involved with either of these repairs, you might want to opt for the complete axle replacement and rest at ease that the problem is remedied.

Insider's Tip

Remind your mechanic if you have ABS (antilock) brakes, as the ABS sensor ring is connected to the axle. The replacement axle must have this ring for the ABS system to work.

"All wheel drive" cars and "rear wheel drive" cars with independent rear suspension have axles with CV joints. Rear-axle CV joints, together with their respective boots, tend to last much longer than the fronts, as they do not have to pivot to steer the car.

Scam Alert

Watch out for a shady mechanic with a razor blade who could quickly slice an axle boot to create a repair job. Remember: A soft, rubbery boot will not just crack. If the boot looks sliced and there is no spin-off of grease around it, you just might have become his next victim.

Body and Fender Repair

Auto body repair and refinishing is an art. Finding an artist to work on your car is not always easy. A good body shop is one that is well equipped with a staff that wants to put out quality work and is willing to go the extra mile to do so. Always convey to the shop owner what your level of expectation is before you authorize the repair. This way he will know in advance that your expectations are high.

Tips Tips
Tips Tips
Tips T
Tips
ps

Insider's Tip

If an insurance company is paying for your repair, have them mail the check directly to you. This will give you added leverage in having complete satisfaction with the repair before the body shop gets paid.

What should you expect from a good body shop?

Ideally you would want your vehicle returned to you in such a condition that you could not tell by looking at it that it was ever damaged. Furthermore, repairs to areas below the surface that you cannot readily see, such as the chassis or unibody, should be accurately and completely performed.

To accomplish professional auto body repair, a body shop must have the right equipment. It should have a modern chassis alignment machine that can stretch and bend the frame of your vehicle back into the proper specifications if they were affected by a collision. It should also have a spray booth, which controls the environment around your vehicle for the refinishing (painting) process. Spray booths are temperature-controlled and have drafts that can minimize the dust that would otherwise fall back onto and into the wet paint. They are well lit, providing the painter with the necessary light to work properly, and they have heat lamps to minimize humidity, which could otherwise adversely affect the paint job.

As with a repair shop, when looking for a body shop always try to find one through a referral and in advance. Look to see if they are registered with the Better Business Bureau or if they are certified by I-CAR (the Inter-Industry Conference on Auto Collision Repair). Use other people's past experiences as a barometer in choosing a good shop. If you have no one to ask, the best way to gauge a shop for proficiency is to be the judge yourself. Pop in and ask to look at some of the work that they have completed. The following is what you should be concerned about when getting your car's body repaired and what you should look for when you pick it up from the body shop:

➤ Body parts should all line up with one another. In other words, the body lines and moldings of the fenders should line up perfectly with the door panels and so forth.

➤ All of the seams (spaces) between the doors, fenders, hood, and trunk should be equal in space.

➤ The hood, trunk, and doors should open and shut smoothly. Check that the windows go up and down smoothly.

➤ Always have your body shop undercoat any exposed metal during the repair process. This will prevent rust from taking hold on bare metal.

➤ The parts of your car that were freshly painted should match not only in color but also in surface texture. Look closely at the paint finish of your car. You might find that the finish is not like glass but instead has an "orange peel" or rippled surface. Compare this to the panels of the vehicle that were just painted. They should match.

➤ The color of the paint should match, and should be viewed both in the shade and in direct sunlight for uniformity. If your paint has metal flakes in it, be sure the flakes match in size and density.

Insider's Tip

Paint suppliers can scan a panel of the car, for instance the gas filler door, to match the paint color.

➤ Keep in mind that a car's finish that has been exposed to the elements over a period of time will fade. So if you paint one panel, such as a door, it will look different than the fender next to it. For this reason you should consider painting entire areas that are viewed together. If only isolated panels are painted, your body shop should "blend" the paint into the adjacent panels to avoid a sharp contrast in the color. Polishing the older faded surfaces with polishing compound will help restore the original finish and reduce or eliminate any shade discrepancies. Remember, using the exact color paint does not always guarantee that the finished product will match. Other factors such as the air pressure at the spray gun, the distance the gun is held from the painted surface, and the reducers or thinners used in the paint will all have an effect on the paint color.

Insider's Tip

Use fluorescent light to reflect off the refinished surface to detect imperfections.

➤ Neatness counts. Look for overspray. Overspray is paint that adheres to surfaces not intended for painting, such as other body panels, moldings, weatherstripping, lenses, glass, and paint that ends up in your trunk or under your hood. When a vehicle is returned to the customer it should be clean inside and out. Dust should be vacuumed and blown out, including the dust that will blow in your face the first time you turn on your heater or air conditioner. Also, a clean car on the outside is important for reviewing and inspecting the finished product. Neatness is a clear indicator that a body shop takes pride in its work.

Insider's Tip

If you come to pay and pick up your car and it is wet from being washed or from the rain, you will not notice any imperfections in the paint or bodywork. Make sure you see the car when it is dry before taking it home.

➤ Insist that moldings, trim, or emblems be removed (as opposed to being taped) before painting. Removal of these parts will ensure proper paint coverage and make for a nicer, cleaner job. Make sure these parts are securely attached when you pick up your vehicle.

➤ Any parts of the body that were not replaced but were repaired with body filler should be closely inspected. First of all, the panel should not be wavy. Large areas of repair are difficult to bring back to factory condition, so allow for minor imperfections. Also, the area should not show any pits or sanding marks.

➤ Replacement parts. Remember that there are options when it comes to parts. The best replacement parts are those that are new and are manufactured by the original equipment manufacturer (OEM)—the car's manufacturer. Then there are aftermarket parts like fenders that are manufactured by companies other than the car manufacturer. These are nice because they are brand-new and less expensive than OEM parts, but they are not made as well and sometimes do not line up perfectly. Other aftermarket parts that are available at discounted prices are tail lenses, mirrors, grilles, fog lights, marker lights, hoods, and more. Your last option would be used parts. These, which are taken off wrecked vehicles, may be in perfect or near-perfect condition. Usually your body shop will be your advocate here in choosing or rejecting parts from a wrecking yard. Your body shop is not going to accept a hood from a wrecker if the hood needs two or three hours of preparation or repair before it can be painted.

Check with your insurance carrier and see what they pay for. If they provide for new OEM parts, demand that the body shop use only OEM parts.

If your airbags were deployed, they must be replaced with "new" not used airbags. Insurance companies and some state regulations require new replacements.

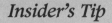

Insider's Tip

If your car was involved in a front-end accident, be sure to check that the radiator and connecting lines are not leaking antifreeze or transmission fluid and check these fluid levels before you pay and drive off with your car. Also be sure to check that the air-conditioning system is working properly, as the air-conditioning condenser may have been damaged and the refrigerant may have leaked out. Finally, your vehicle's headlights may have been knocked out of their proper alignment and may need to be adjusted. Check them against a wall at night to see if they are even.

Insider's Tip

Remember that body shops sometimes work with their customers to cover insurance "deductibles." They are willing to absorb the deductible cost of their customer if the repair job is extensive. Try to negotiate this before the work is started. Beware that if the deductible is very high and the shop agrees to cover it, they might try to cut corners on the repair to make it worthwhile to them. They can do this by using used or aftermarket parts.

Brakes, Rotors, and Calipers

The brake system is made up of many parts, some of which may need to be replaced after time and usage.

The brakes of a car work by slowing down the spinning wheels as they turn. This is accomplished through friction.

The system works as follows: When you apply foot pressure to the brake pedal you are pressing a rod and plunger in a master cylinder that pressurizes the brake fluid. This pressure is enhanced by the power booster. The pressurized brake fluid passes through brake lines and brake hoses into calipers (disc brakes) or wheel cylinders (drum brakes), which expand under the pressure. This in turn forces the brake pads against the rotors or drums that are attached to the spinning wheels of the car. This causes friction between these pads and the rotors and drums, causing them to slow down.

So what wears out?

Depending on the vehicle, the driver, and the frequency of stopping, front brake pads need to be replaced after approximately 20,000 miles. Rear pads or drum brake shoes usually outlast the front ones because they do not work as hard when stopping. In the event that your brake pads wear out completely, you will hear a grinding "metal to metal" sound on braking. The reason the pads, which are made from heat-resistant material, need to be replaced is because the pad material slowly wears thin. Most pads have wear indicators—metal tabs that scrape the brake rotor disc, causing a loud squeak and calling attention to the brakes. Some cars have sensors that will set off a light on the dashboard.

Note: If your brake pads or shoes wear thin, replace them before they damage the rotors or drums. Damage is caused when the brake material completely wears out from the tremendous amount of heat and friction produced from braking. Once the brake material wears out, the metal base of the brake pad grinds into the metal rotor disc, destroying it.

You can ask to see the worn, thin pads and compare them to new, thick pads to see the contrast between them.

Scam Alert

During an inspection of the brake pads or brake shoes, an unscrupulous mechanic could wedge his screwdriver between the brake material and the metal support and crack off a section or corner. Without the resources of a forensics laboratory it would be hard to prove this. This is why it is very important to find a shop that you feel confident in.

The brake rotors, which are the round metal discs that are squeezed by the brake pads, should be replaced as follows:

A. When the excessively worn-out brake pads have gouged them.

B. When they have developed fine lines in them.

C. When they are warped from high temperature, causing the car to slow down with a head-jerking motion or a pulsating feeling in the brake pedal.

D. When they have worn thin from normal wear and tear.

Rotors and drums can be shaved down (resurfaced) when they develop fine lines or mild grooves in them, to re-create a smooth and true surface. However, new rotors and drums are the smart choice.

Sometimes the other components of the brake system fail. They need to be replaced as follows:

A. When the master cylinder allows the brake pedal to sink to the floor or when it leaks brake fluid.

B. When the power booster develops a crack in its internal diaphragm and the brake pedal becomes rock-hard.

C. When the brake hoses become dry-rotted and crack or leak.

D. When the brake calipers leak or when they fail to release, causing the wheel to lock or drag. *Note:* Drive your car for ten minutes and stop a dozen times, then place your hand close to the wheel on each tire. If one wheel is hotter than the rest, then that wheel is dragging due to a locked caliper. A burning smell usually accompanies the heated wheel.

E. When the wheel cylinder (drum brakes) leaks.

F. When brake hardware such as cables or springs break or wear out.

Remember, your car's brakes can mean the difference between life and death. Always have an experienced technician inspect and repair your vehicle's brakes.

ANTILOCK BRAKES (ABS)

Antilock brake systems (ABS), which were first introduced in 1992 on the American market, were designed to maintain steering and lateral control capabilities under extreme stopping conditions, by detecting when one or more wheels stops rolling or skids during braking. A skidding or sliding tire or tires extends the stopping distance of the vehicle and compromises its ability to steer.

When the onboard ABS computer detects that a wheel or wheels are locked up, it rapidly pulsates that particular caliper or wheel cylinder, causing that wheel to unlock while at the same time slowing it down. This pulsating creates a bumpy sensation on the brake pedal.

Unfortunately, many people I have spoken to tend to drive faster in the rain and snow because they feel more confident in their ability to stop faster under these conditions. The truth of the matter is that when the traction coefficient between the road and the tires disappears, the vehicle will still lose control of stopping and steering. Snow and rain should always be a reason to slow down the pace.

The most common problems with ABS systems involve the wheel speed sensors or broken or damaged wheel sensor rings. Either will cause the ABS warning light to illuminate. Moisture that is absorbed into the brake fluid can corrode hydraulic valves and valve seats in the ABS system. A litmus test can be done on the brake fluid to determine if it needs to be replaced due to moisture.

Tips Tips
Tips
ips T
Tip
ps

Insider's Tip

One different-size (overall circumference) tire can trigger your ABS warning light.

Tips Tips
Tips
ips T
Tip

Insider's Tip

If you spin one tire while your car is on the lift with the ignition on, it could trigger your ABS light to illuminate.

If the ABS warning light should come on, the vehicle should be diagnosed at your car dealership or by a qualified ABS technician. There are a number of components, from sensors to ABS pumps, that can go bad. An experienced technician with the right diagnostic equipment can pinpoint specific problems with this system!

Tips Tips
Tips
ips T
Tip

Insider's Tip

To keep your ABS system working properly you should engage it from time to time. To do this, go to an area free from other cars or people on a rainy or snowy day. Drive approximately 25 mph and press forcefully on the brakes. You should feel a bumpy sensation in the brake pedal together with an unusual noise. Do this a few times and repeat periodically to keep all of the moving parts of your ABS system in good working order.

Catalytic Converters

Catalytic converters are mounted on the exhaust system. Exhaust gases pass through the catalytic converter before they are released into the atmosphere. A catalyst is a device that promotes a chemical reaction without itself being changed or consumed by the chemical process. In the case of the exhaust gases produced by your vehicle's internal combustion engine, the catalytic converter changes the harmful pollutants into harmless ones, making the air we breathe cleaner while protecting the earth's ozone layer.

Catalytic converters usually go bad as a result of the engine running poorly, which could be the result of engine misfire or incorrect air/fuel ratio. An improper fuel octane rating for your vehicle will prematurely ruin your catalytic converter. Cars and light trucks produced for the U.S. since 1996 have an onboard computer system called OBD-II, which not only monitors the performance of various components and subsystems but also makes adjustments necessary to protect the cat.

Catalytic converters are protected by federal law, which states that auto manufacturers must extend their warranties on catalytic converters for eight years or 80,000 miles on 1995 and newer vehicles. For more information on this, visit the federal Environmental Protection Agency's Web site at www.epa.gov/otaq/consumer/warr95fs.txt. If your catalytic converter had been changed before with an aftermarket part, that part would have a two-year, 24,000-mile warranty from the manufacturer.

If your vehicle develops a "shushing" noise similar to that of pressurized air escaping through a hole, have your car checked out. It may be clogged and restricting the exhaust. This might be accompanied by a loss of power on acceleration.

Check Engine Lights/Codes

As technology evolves it is applied to the modern-day cars we drive. Vehicles and light trucks employ onboard computer systems that monitor and control more and more functions, ranging from emission control–related systems to transmission systems. It would be pointless to delve into the belly of the beast with every system, but the following is what you really need to know.

If your check engine light (or MIL—malfunction indicator light) comes on and stays on, it is an indication that a sensor (for example, an emissions system sensor) has been triggered. Starting in 1996, all cars and light trucks sold in the USA were upgraded from OBD-I (onboard diagnostic generation one) to OBD-II (generation two). OBD-II can detect the deterioration of emission controls or powertrain components by running several test functions. These tests will detect, for instance, higher than normal exhaust emission levels and will trigger your check engine light, or MIL, to stay on.

If this light comes on, don't panic. It will need to be addressed but it does not require immediate attention, unlike an oil pressure, overheating, or alternator light, which does.

Take your vehicle to a shop that specializes in auto diagnostics. If the light starts flashing on and off, severe catalytic converter damage and power loss will occur soon. More immediate service is required. With the right equipment and personnel, your vehicle can be diagnosed and repaired properly, and not simply by the process of elimination. (Extended driving with the check engine light on could damage the catalytic converter.)

If the technician finds a DTC (diagnostic trouble code), ask him to guarantee that he can repair the problem, clear the code and the light on your dashboard, and stand behind the repair.

Sophisticated computer systems can be troublesome when they go on the blink, but the point of such systems is to keep your engine working at its optimum efficiency with minimal harmful emissions. The illuminated MIL is simply letting you know that something is not right. A technician's job is to pinpoint the problem using a scanner and his training and to correct it.

Sometimes even as simple a thing as not tightening the gas cap after refueling or running the engine while refueling can trigger the check engine light. Disconnecting your battery for a brief period will sometimes clear the light, but be prepared to reprogram your clock and radio. Some anti-theft radios need to be programmed with a code number, so make sure you have this number beforehand.

Exhaust System/Muffler

The exhaust system carries burnt fuel in the form of gases from the engine. They pass through the exhaust manifold into a pipe, through a catalytic converter, and finally through the muffler and tailpipe.

What can go bad and how will you know it?

Let's start from the source. The engine produces exhaust gases that are pushed into the exhaust manifolds. There are gaskets

Insider's Tip

Most car manufacturers offer bumper-to-bumper warranties of at least three years or 36,000 miles, which would include emission-related problems. In addition, the federal government has protected consumers by implementing a law that requires car manufacturers to extend their warranties on three major components—catalytic converters, electronic control units (ECUs), and onboard diagnostic devices (OBDs). These components are covered for eight years or 80,000 miles on 1995 or newer vehicles. For more information on this, visit the federal Environmental Protection Agency's Web site at www.epa.gov/otaq/consumer/warr95fs.txt.

between the engine and the manifolds. Seldom do they blow out, but if they do there will be a loud rhythmic sound made by the engine.

After the manifolds, the gases go down an engine pipe and into a catalytic converter. Converters typically do not leak exhaust, but they can clog and restrict the flow of exhaust. (Refer to the "Catalytic Converters" section on page 23.) Beyond the converter is a connecting pipe that leads into the muffler, which reduces the sound created by the fuel as it burns in the engine's cylinders. It is similar to a large can with a series of chambers that deaden the sound. From the muffler the exhaust passes through a tailpipe in the rear of the car, where it exits the system. (Some vehicles have a resonator in the exhaust system that further muffles the sound of the exhaust.)

The muffler, the exhaust pipes, and the gaskets that seal the connections between these parts are subjected to pressure, moisture, rust, and road salt. In addition to this, hot and cold temperatures, expansion, contraction, and metal fatigue take their toll on the exhaust system. Short trips, especially on cold days, leave a lot of condensation in the system. The pipes never get hot enough or stay hot enough to evaporate this water, which combines with sulfur from the exhaust, creating a highly corrosive acid. This acid then eats away at the exhaust system. The parts of the system that are at the tail end of the car suffer from this reaction the most as they tend not to get as hot as the front of the system.

Car manufacturers treat their exhaust systems to prevent corrosion, and they usually last about five years under good conditions.

How would one know if something was broken or about to break? One symptom of a faulty exhaust would be a loud "motorboat" sound. If any part of the exhaust system develops a leak, it will create a loud sound, generally getting louder as the engine revs faster. If your car seems or is louder than usual, have the exhaust checked for leaks or breaks, and replace the faulty parts.

Visual inspection: Whenever your car is on a lift, the exhaust system should be visually inspected for wear. Surface rust is common and nothing to be deeply concerned about, but corroded parts should be replaced. Corroded pipes can easily be squeezed with channel lock pliers to determine if they are ready to collapse. In addition, the hangers from which the exhaust system is suspended should be checked for cracks or wear and tear. Mufflers typically have a small hole built into them at a low point for drainage of condensation.

Mufflers can be damaged as a result of engine backfire, which collapses and distorts their original shape. They are not guaranteed against this type of failure because it is caused by the engine backfiring and not because of a faulty muffler. They may also be in need of replacement because of a faulty catalytic converter, which may leak its pellets back into the muffler, causing it to restrict or completely block the flow of exhaust.

Mufflers and catalytic converters can also break internally so that the chambers become dislodged inside. An internal rattle will be an indication of a broken muffler or catalytic converter.

Sometimes exhaust parts cannot be changed independently of one another because they are manufactured as one piece from the automaker. For instance, if your original muffler needs to be replaced, you might also need to replace the connecting pipe or the tailpipe because they are all welded together. There are some muffler shops or repair shops that can cut out individual parts and weld or clamp new ones in, but many shops would prefer to sell you the entire system.

Exhaust systems vary a great deal in quality, so insist on name brands and look for lifetime guarantees. Ask for direct fit parts, which are designed to fit your specific make and model, as opposed to universal parts that have to be manipulated to fit. Keep in mind that many vehicles have a part known as a flex pipe. This pipe is designed to flex a little without breaking, thus allowing the engine to pivot without stressing and cracking the pipe, which extends from the engine. Typically flex pipes break because the engine's motor mounts break. The engine in turn pivots excessively, causing the flex pipe to crack. A new flex pipe is very expensive because it comes as one piece from the dealer or supplier, sometimes with the catalytic converter built into it. Replacing the flex pipe is very expensive, but most muffler shops or independent shops can weld in a new one without replacing the entire piece.

Insider's Tip

Sometimes plastic bags from the street adhere (melt) themselves to your car's exhaust system, resulting in a burning odor. They will in time melt off or can be scraped off the next time the car is on a lift. Don't worry if this occurs. It poses no harm to the driver or the vehicle.

Fuel Injection

Fuel injection was introduced back in the 1950s, but for many years carburetors remained the primary method of feeding fuel to car engines.

Today, however, all cars employ fuel injection systems. These are very sophisticated and use computers together with sensors to deliver the proper amount of fuel and air to the combustion chamber. Such a system produces the most energy with the least amount of pollution and takes into consideration all of the vehicle's operating conditions. Fuel injection, when working properly, is very efficient.

If your vehicle develops operating or starting problems, it could very well be related to one of the many fuel injection components. Unfortunately, a skilled technician will have to diagnose the problem.

Insider's Tip

There are fuel injector cleaners available at all auto parts stores that can be added to the fuel to help clean dirty fuel injectors. In addition, there is a professional system that cleans the injectors at the injector by using a pressurized canister filled with a solvent. This way is most effective.

Glass and Locks

Certain specialty shops specialize in the repair or replacement of specific parts. They include:

➤ Windshields. They are available new, used, or aftermarket.

Insider's Tip

Always keep a close eye on your windshield after it has been replaced, as stress cracks can develop from improper installation.

➤ Door glass. Also available new, used, or aftermarket. Aftermarket glass, like many other products, comes in higher and lower grades. Ask for the best or OEM.

Insider's Tip

Allow sufficient time for the glue, which should be urethane, to dry. Silicone, which is prohibited by law for sealing windshields, should not be used. And always check for water leaks inside your vehicle after the windshield has been replaced.

➤ Window regulators. The mechanical track or mechanism needed to raise or lower your window.

➤ Steering columns. This includes any part attached to or related to your steering column. Only allow technicians who are experts in steering column repair to perform any service on the column.

➤ Door key cylinders. The cylinders needed to lock and unlock your car from the outside. *Note:* Lubricate the cylinders periodically.

➤ Power windows. The power window motor or any electrical part like the P/W switch or relay. *Note:* Lubricate the window channels with a silicone spray periodically.

➤ Power door locks. Includes parts such as switches or solenoids.

➤ Keying locks. The matching of a lock cylinder to a specific existing key so as not to need more than one key to open doors and to start the car.

➤ Alarm systems. The repair and installation of a wide variety of alarm systems.

Insider's Tip

Dealerships cannot void your car's warranty because your alarm or stereo was installed elsewhere.

➤ Remote start systems. The installation of a remote-controlled starter to enable you to start your car from a distance. *Warning:* Never install such a system on a vehicle with a manual transmission, as the car might be started while in gear.

➤ Stereo systems. Includes stereo systems, CD changers, speakers, amplifiers, etc.

➤ Electric antennas. Includes power antenna motors or their masts.

➤ Ignition cylinders. The repair or replacement of ignition cylinders that have failed from wear and tear or from vandalism or car theft.

Leaks

What leaks? From where? What should I do about it?

Other than actually seeing something dripping, one indicator of a leaking condition is when you have to keep adding a particular fluid. If you have to add fluid, it must be going somewhere. Is it going into thin air? It just might be. Oil, transmission fluid (on vacuum operated modules), and antifreeze can find their way into the combustion chamber, where they are burnt. You would never see a drip in this case, but if you do not see excessive smoke coming out of your exhaust pipe, wipe the tailpipe with a paper towel and check for the presence of an oily residue.

One other level (measurement) will go down without an actual leak. That would be the brake fluid. When your brake pads and brake shoes wear thin, the hydraulic pistons in the calipers extend, drawing brake fluid into them. This lowers the brake fluid level in the master cylinder reservoir, giving the impression that there might be a leak. When new brake pads are installed, the pistons and the calipers are pressed back in, causing the fluid to be pressurized back up into the reservoir.

The different fluids that are found in your automobile are as follows:

1. Engine oil

2. Automatic transmission fluid

3. Manual transmission oil

4. Antifreeze

5. Power steering fluid

6. Brake fluid

7. Rear end (differential) oil

8. Windshield washer fluid

9. Transfer case (four-wheel drive)

1. **Engine oil** can leak from many places on the engine. There are many gaskets and seals that can leak oil. Sometimes the leak is profuse, making its source obvious. Other times the leak may be small and spread over large areas of the engine, which can make it more difficult to pinpoint. If this is the case, have the engine steam-cleaned to remove all residual oil and grime. Then run the engine for a period of time and visually check for a fresh source of leaking oil. Replace the gasket or seal accordingly.

Frequent sources of motor oil leakage include the oil drain plug, oil filter, or oil sender switch. The drain plug and oil filter are removed every time you change your oil. Check to make sure that the filter is on firmly and that the drain plug gasket is not worn out.

The oil sender switch signals the oil pressure gauge or pressure light on your dashboard. This switch, which is usually located near the oil filter, is under oil pressure and frequently leaks. It is an easy and inexpensive part to replace.

If your engine is equipped with a PCV (positive crankcase ventilation) valve, check or change it with each tune-up, as a clogged PCV valve can cause oil leaks to develop.

Finally, there are oil treatments available on the market that swell rubber seals, causing them to fit tighter and seal leaks. Replacing a worn seal or gasket with a new one is always the best way to fix a leak, but if the job is too costly for your wallet, try the oil treatment.

2. **Automatic transmission fluid** is pink and is easy to identify. ATF typically leaks from the gaskets or seals on the transmission. Some of these are easily accessible, but some are not. If the job requires removing the transmission, consider adding a sealant into the transmission fluid.

Transmission fluid is cooled in the radiator. Some leaks develop in the lines that connect to the radiator. Check these lines, their connections, and the radiator for leaks.

It is sometimes necessary to wash down the transmission to pinpoint a leak.

3. **Manual transmission oil** is usually honey-colored, heavy, and smelly. It is a heavyweight oil, generally about 80–90 weight, and is designed to lubricate gears that are subjected to heavy pressures. Manual transmissions, not unlike automatic transmissions, can leak from seals or gaskets, in which case they must be replaced. If they leak, replace them. Manual transmissions do not have dipsticks to check the oil level. They must be checked by opening a filler bolt on the side of the transmission.

Note: if a leak is not serious, it may be more cost-effective to just add more fluid as needed.

4. **Antifreeze** can leak from a variety of places, including: (a) the radiator, (b) the water pump, (c) the heater core, (d) the radiator hoses, (e) the heater hoses, (f) the heater control valve, (g) the head gaskets, (h) the overflow bottle, and (i) the radiator cap.

Identifying an antifreeze leak is usually easy. For one thing, it is either green or maroon. When the engine is hot or overheating it generally steams out. And it is very fluid, like water, so it runs down.

If the leak is too minute to find, have your mechanic pressure test the system. This pressure buildup forces antifreeze out of the leak at a higher rate, making it more visible.

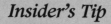
If you find that you have to add antifreeze and you cannot locate any leaks, your engine might be burning it or it may be leaking into the crankcase. Either scenario would be due to a blown head gasket or a crack in the head or engine block. Check your engine oil for clouding (milky) oil. If your oil dipstick comes out white and the level is high, chances are you have blown a head gasket.

Leaks from the radiator, hoses, heater core, and water pump will require replacement of the offender. Quick fixes like cooling system sealants do work much of the time, but new is new. New radiators can be purchased from the manufacturer (dealer) or from an aftermarket company. These aftermarket radiators have worked well for me.

Note: Heater cores are small radiators that disperse heat into the passenger compartment. When they leak or get clogged, they need to be replaced. Even a small leak from the heater core will produce a fog on the inside of your lower windshield. Replacement usually requires extensive labor under the dashboard. For this problem I would recommend a radiator shop that does this type of work on a regular basis.

5. **Power steering fluid** can leak from the following places: (a) the power steering pump, (b) the high- or low-pressure hoses, (c) the rack and pinion, or (d) the steering box.

The power steering pump pressurizes fluid, creating power-assisted steering. This pump can leak from a seal, a gasket, or the filler cap. The hoses that lead from the pump to the steering box or rack and pinion are subject to leaks also. Usually the high-pressure hose (not the return hose) is the culprit.

Most cars today have rack-and-pinion steering systems as opposed to steering boxes. Racks have seals at either end that sometimes fail and leak.

Cars that have steering boxes usually develop leaks at the pinion seal. This seal can usually be replaced without removing the steering box.

Power steering fluid is usually pink like transmission fluid. In some cases transmission fluid is used as power steering fluid. Treatments are available to combat leaks in the power steering system, but leaks that develop under pressure usually require new seals or gaskets.

Scam Alert

A shady mechanic can drip or spray oil onto a part to simulate a leak. Keep this in mind whenever your car goes up on a lift.

6. **Brake fluid** leaks are serious. They indicate a failure in a system that is crucial in stopping your vehicle. (Refer to the "Brakes, Rotors, and Calipers" section on page 19.)

Caution: Brake fluid will damage your paint, so take measures to protect it in the event of a spill or spray.

➤ Always replace worn or leaking components of the brake system.

➤ Never add anything but the prescribed type of DOT (Department of Transportation) brake fluid to the system.

➤ If oil or transmission fluid is accidentally added to the system, have it bled completely and checked by a service technician for possible swelling of the rubber parts. *Replace* any parts that have been compromised.

The hydraulic parts of the brake system are:

1. The master cylinder reservoir

2. The master cylinder

3. The brake lines

4. The proportioning valve

5. The brake hoses

6. The ABS pump

7. The brake calipers

8. The wheel cylinders

If any of these components develops a leak, have it replaced immediately. In addition to leaks, brake hoses can collapse internally, restricting the flow of brake fluid. Externally they sometimes develop cracks due to dry rot. If cracks in the hoses are visible, it is time to replace all of them.

7. **Rear end oil, or differential oil,** tends to leak out from either the pinion seal or axle seals. When it leaks from the pinion seal it drips onto the end of the driveshaft, where it spins off onto the underside of the car, leaving its mark. When it leaks from the axle seals, it drips down into the brake drum, usually saturating the brake shoes with oil.

If you notice that the inner side of your tire is wet and shiny, chances are the axle seal (or brake wheel cylinder) is leaking. Remove the wheel and inspect.

8. **Windshield washer fluid**, which is blue, can leak from (a) the reservoir tank, (b) the washer pump, or (c) the hoses that carry

the fluid to the windshield. Make sure to use washer solvent, especially in the winter, as water in the system will freeze and crack parts.

A leaking reservoir tank can usually be patched with epoxy cement. A leaking pump must be replaced unless it is leaking from the connecting gasket. Hoses that have popped off can be snipped at their ends and reattached, and then pressurized air can be blown through the hoses to clear them. If the obstruction is in the washer outlet, try a fine pin in the orifice to clear it.

9. The **transfer case** on four-wheel-drive vehicles contains the gears necessary to propel an additional driveshaft. This shaft connects to the front differential propelling the front wheels of a four-wheel-drive vehicle. The gears in the transfer case are lubricated either by transmission fluid or a heavyweight oil, usually 90 weight (90W). The transfer case can develop leaks through its gaskets or seals. Have your mechanic inspect for leaks and periodically check the fluid levels.

Oil and the Oil Filter

The main purpose of oil is to minimize friction between moving parts that would otherwise rub directly against each other under pressure, causing them to fail. An engine has many moving parts that spin fast and do so under extreme pressure and at extreme temperatures. These moving parts include but are not limited to: the crankshaft, the connecting rods, the pistons, the camshafts, the timing chain, and the valvetrain. These main parts and others not only need to be constantly lubricated, they also need to be lubricated under pressure, which forms a cushion between the parts. This pressure is provided by the oil pump. The pressurized oil is pumped through channels throughout the engine, and these passageways must remain clean and unobstructed.

Not only does oil lubricate, it also provides other benefits to your engine. It absorbs heat from the mechanical parts of the engine and then dissipates the heat when it passes through the oil pan. Some oil pans have fins molded into them to facilitate the transfer of heat out into the air.

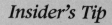

Insider's Tip

Many shops advertise brand-name oils. This oil is often purchased in bulk and is dispensed out of a bulk tank. You can ask to see the last delivery invoice to verify that you are getting the name-brand oil as opposed to an inferior or recycled oil.

Most oils have a detergent agent in them that washes the inside of the engine, picking up moisture, acid, and particles that are by-products of the combustion chamber. Changing your oil is one way of removing these contaminants.

Changing your oil and the oil filter (which traps and removes small and large particles from circulating in your engine) regularly will prevent your engine from wearing out prematurely. It will cut down on friction, increase performance, and lower fuel consumption. Your car will pollute less and your engine will last longer.

Change your oil and filter at 3,000–4,000-mile intervals, more often if you drive hard, tow a vehicle, or if you have high mileage. Some vehicles require the use of synthetic oils. (Refer to the "Synthetic Oils" section on page 39.) Check under the hood for a decal or check your owner's manual.

Changing your oil and filter yourself is not extremely difficult, but you should consider the risk, the mess, and the proper disposal of the dirty oil.

Insider's Tip

Remember that when you first start your engine after it has been sitting for a while (dry starts), the oil will be sitting in the oil pan. That means that it first needs to circulate before it can protect. If this is the case, do not rev the engine or drive the car without letting it warm up.

Other facts about oil:

➤ Oils have different designations of weight. The heavier weight oil has a higher number, and its ability to flow is less than oil with a lower weight number, which is thinner and flows and pours faster.

➤ Multigrade oil (e.g., 5W-30) works well across a wide range of temperatures. The lower the first number, the easier the oil will flow on cold days. As the oil warms up it will then offer the protection of a thicker grade of oil.

➤ Single-viscosity oil (e.g., 40W) will be most effective where the climate is steady. Be sure to use the right grade of oil if you choose to use a single-viscosity oil.

➤ If your car drips or consumes a lot of oil, repair the problem, but be sure not to run your engine on a low oil level. A low level of oil in your oil pan becomes sludgy after a short while and will not be able to properly lubricate your engine.

CHECK YOUR OIL DIPSTICK ON A REGULAR BASIS.

Insider's Tip

An oil lube job has become an oil and oil filter change without the lube, as most cars are manufactured with pre-greased, sealed front-end components (tie rods, idler arms, ball joints) that cannot accept grease.

SYNTHETIC OILS

Should I use synthetic oil over petroleum-based oil?

Here are the facts:

Synthetic oils offer superior resistance to high temperatures. They will not oxidize or burn easily. On the other end of the spectrum, they offer better protection to your engine under extremely cold temperatures.

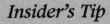

If you drive a high-performance engine, a turbo- or super-charged engine, or tow with your vehicle, especially in extremely hot climates, your vehicle will benefit from synthetic oil. If you live in an extremely cold climate, synthetic oil is the right choice, as it provides faster upper valvetrain lubrication on cold starts, which is when most engine wear occurs. This is especially important with vehicles with overhead camshafts.

Other advantages to using synthetic oil are:

➤ Longer oil change intervals. This might be especially attractive for people who live in the fast lane and cannot make time for their 3,000–4,000-mile oil change with conventional oil. Synthetic oil resists viscosity (the ability to lubricate) breakdown and oxidation, which extends the life of the oil up to even 15,000 miles between oil changes. However, short trips together with cold weather increase the amount of moisture that collects in the crankcase, so do not push it till 15,000. Another thing to consider is that you might be waiving your vehicle manufacturer's warranty by not changing your oil at their recommended intervals.

➤ Slightly better fuel economy, as these oils are more slippery than petroleum-based oils and therefore create less friction.

➤ It is true that synthetic oil is more expensive, but consider the longer intervals between oil changes and the reduced costs of engine repair and maintenance. These factors, together with longer engine life, might prove to be cost-effective in the long run. Should you choose to accumulate high mileage between oil changes on synthetic oil, you should change the oil filter every 7,000 miles to help keep the oil clean and flowing.

Synthetic oil is compatible with petroleum-based oil and can be added to your regular oil for added protection.

Synthetic blends are also available for purchase at a marginal cost. These are mixtures of synthetic and mineral-based oil that are less effective than pure synthetic but more effective than petroleum-based oil.

Overheating

One of the most common reasons an engine overheats is because the radiator fan does not spin. Older cars have fans that are driven by a fan belt attached to the spinning engine via a pulley system. This system usually incorporates a fan clutch that is designed to slip when the engine is cold and grab as the engine warms up. When the fan clutch wears out, the fan slips, even when hot, and loses its ability to draw air through the radiator, causing the engine to run hot or even overheat. A qualified mechanic can determine if this is the case.

Later-model cars use electric radiator fans. These are activated by a sensor triggered when the engine exceeds its normal operating temperature. If this sensor or the relay switch that connects the sensor to the fan motor fails, the fan will not turn on and the engine will overheat. If the engine is overheating and the fan motor is not working, check the fuse. It may be blown. This system is more fuel-efficient because it does not drag or impose any strain on the engine itself.

Caution: Never touch the fan blades, even with the engine off.

Overheating can occur due to some obvious reasons. A hole in the radiator or any of the radiator hoses will cause the antifreeze to spray out. Bugs or leaves trapped between the air-conditioning condenser and the radiator will restrict the flow of air to the radiator, which will not only cause the engine to run hot but will also compromise the air-conditioning system.

Warning: Continued driving even for a short period of time when the engine is overheated can damage the engine. Heads that are aluminum can warp from the extreme heat and/or the head gaskets can blow. Either scenario would be expensive to repair, so avoid driving if the needle goes into the red or the temperature light stays on.

UNDERHEATING

Some vehicles blow cool or lukewarm air from their heaters in the wintertime. Other vehicles take a long time to warm up or never do reach the proper operating temperature, which is about 180–190 degrees Fahrenheit.

If this is the case, open your radiator cap (when the engine is cold) and see if you are low on coolant. If you are, top off the radiator and overflow bottle with antifreeze. Start the engine. Many cars that are low on coolant will not be able to produce sufficient heat.

If this process is to no avail, the next step would be to check to see if the thermostat is stuck in the open position. This test must be performed with a cold engine. Loosen the upper radiator hose clamp and twist the upper hose off the radiator. Start the vehicle. If the antifreeze starts pumping out of the hose, it would indicate that the thermostat is stuck open or it was previously removed. If this is the case, replace the thermostat and gasket, top off the fluid, and check the heater. It should start to produce heat after about five minutes, depending on the outside temperature.

Another possible cause of insufficient heat in the car would be because the radiator's electric fan stays on constantly. The fan should kick on only after the engine exceeds its operating temperature. It then stays on only long enough to cool down the coolant and then the cycle begins again. If the fan comes on as soon as you start your cold engine, it will take a long time for your car to heat up inside. Check to ensure that your control settings are in the heat position and not in the A/C or defroster position, as these latter two positions will cause the electric radiator fans to stay on constantly.

Caution: DO NOT TOUCH the fan blade as the fan can self-activate.

Another possible cause of weak heat could be a faulty heater control valve. The heater control valve opens and shuts in reaction to the control setting on your dashboard. If it does not open, hot coolant cannot enter into the heater core and heat will be a "no show."

Lastly, if the heater core is clogged or partially clogged with scaly rust, heating up your car will become next to impossible. Reverse flushing of the heater core may remove sediment, but if it is severely clogged it will have to be replaced in order to produce sufficient heat.

Starting Problems

You get into your car, put the key into the ignition, and turn it. The darn car is not starting! What should you do? There are steps to be taken to determine why it is not starting.

First, notice whether your dome light works when the door is open and, if it does, is it as bright as normal. Second, see whether your dashboard gauges and warning (red) lights come on when the key is turned to the on position just before the cranking or starting position. Third, crank or start the engine by turning the ignition key all the way. What happens? Your choices are:

1. Nothing—no sound

2. Fast cranking or spinning of the engine, but no starting

3. Slow cranking, which sounds like a slow-motion winding noise

4. Rapid clicking

5. One loud click each time the ignition key is turned

6. Grinding

1. **Nothing—no sound.** If there is no evidence of any power to either the dome lights, headlights, or dashboard lights and gauges, then there is no power coming into the car. This could be because the battery is completely dead, or is missing (stolen), or, most commonly, has a bad connection. First locate the battery and see if it has a power indicator eye. If so, it should be green, indicating the battery is okay. If it is not green, the battery is probably dead.

Warning: When working near or touching batteries, exercise caution, as batteries contain sulfuric acid and can burn skin, eyes, and clothing. Batteries can also explode.

Bad connection? Put the headlights to the on position, pop the hood, and get out and look at the headlights. If they are not on, grip one of the battery cables where it connects to the battery terminal and jiggle it. If the lights come on even momentarily then you have located your bad battery connection. Clean (with hot water and baking soda mixed together) and/or tighten the connection with a wrench. If jiggling of the cable end is to no avail, try this step on the other terminal. If this does not help, get a boost from another car or charge your battery on a battery charger. (Refer to the "When to Jump-Start a Car and How" section on page 48.)

Tip: Make sure your car is in park or neutral and the clutch pedal is down (if applicable).

2. **Fast cranking or spinning of the engine, but no starting.** If the car shows signs of life, like strong headlights, horn, dash lights and gauges, and the engine cranks fast but does not start at all, we know that the battery and starter motor are functioning. What we do not know at this point is why the engine is not starting, which could be due to a host of different reasons. Due to the vast array of possibilities, it would be prudent to call on the professionals for help. But if you want to look further by yourself, you would want to check the following: that there is gas in your tank; that the fuse for the fuel pump is not blown (refer to the owner's manual). Also check to see if your car has a fuel cutoff switch in the trunk (Ford/Mercury products). This switch is a circuit breaker that "pops" if the car is in an accident, so as not to continue to pump fuel and "fuel the fire." These switches sometimes pop if the car is tapped by another car, which can happen while driving or even when the car is parked.

The engine cranking but not starting can be caused by a condition known as "no spark." This is when the spark plugs are not receiving spark from the ignition system. To determine whether or not your spark plugs are receiving the necessary spark needed to start your engine, follow this procedure:

1. Locate any of the ignition wires going from the distributor to the spark plugs.

2. Slowly twist and pull the ignition wire boot off any spark plug.

3. Insert a screwdriver into the boot end, contacting the metal clip in the boot with the end of the screwdriver.

4. Hold the plastic or wood screwdriver handle and place the metal shaft of the screwdriver about one-quarter inch away from any metal part of the engine.

5. Have someone else try to start the engine while you look for a spark to jump (bridge) from the screwdriver to the engine. *Caution:* The ignition coil produces high voltage, which will jolt you if you come in contact with the shaft of the screwdriver or the spark. Use extreme caution when performing this procedure and also be aware of other moving parts in the engine compartment during this procedure. *Beware:* Do not attempt this procedure on newer ignition systems, as it could damage both the system and the person.

If you see a spark jump from the screwdriver to the engine (through the air gap of one-quarter inch), it is safe to assume your spark plugs are getting "spark." If you do not see any spark, this would indicate that your vehicle could have an ignition-related problem. It could be a faulty crank sensor, coil, magnetic pickup, ignition module, or a host of other possibilities. It will take a skilled technician to pinpoint and repair this problem.

If the engine sounds like it is cranking extremely fast but it is not starting, it could be that your timing belt has snapped or jumped teeth. This condition would leave your intake and exhaust valves out of sequence with the movement of the pistons, causing the engine to crank or spin without compression. The lack of compression would allow the starter motor to spin the engine with less compression or backpressure, causing it to spin very fast. If this is the case, nothing short of a new timing belt will get you going again. On "interference engines" the valves are likely to be damaged when the timing belt breaks. If this happens, a very major repair of your engine will be necessary.

3. **Slow cranking, which sounds like a slow-motion winding noise.** Slow cranking is usually due to a weak and almost dead battery. Generally it is followed by (4.) **rapid clicking.** A weak battery will usually have enough juice to honk your horn, raise your window, and turn on your radio, but it takes a lot of energy to start your engine.

A weak battery can be the result of quite a few different problems. First of all, your battery can become weak or dead as a result of non-charging. It is the job of the alternator to replenish the battery with electricity. If the alternator stops functioning properly, the battery will go dead. An indicator light should illuminate if the alternator stops doing its job. If your car is equipped with a gauge, the needle in the gauge will go into the discharge area. The gauge should indicate about 14.2 volts when charging properly.

If the indicator light, which would read "battery" or "alternator," illuminates or your gauge needle goes south, the first thing to check is your alternator or serpentine belt. This belt drives (spins) the alternator. If it should break or become loose, the alternator will stop recharging the battery. With the engine off, test the tension of the alternator belt. It should not have any slack in it. If it does, have it tightened. Some serpentine belts (appropriately named because they snake through a maze of pulleys) are self-adjusting through a spring-loaded tensioner. If the tensioner goes bad, the belt will have slack and the alternator, among other accessories, will not function properly.

A weak battery is due to either old age (usually after three years), cold temperatures, frequent starts, a "short" or "drain" (a condition that drains the battery even when the car is off), a dome light or other light left on after the engine was shut off, or overcharging (when the alternator's regulator allows too much

Scam Alert

If a technician wants to show you that the reading on his voltmeter is showing low and that your alternator is not putting out the proper voltage (between 13.6 and 14.2 volts), check that the meter needle is set at dead zero when it is not hooked up to your car's battery. Like any scale, it can be tampered with. If he sets the needle to negative one before he tests your alternator, the gauge will indicate a low voltage output and he will try to sell you an alternator job.

current into the battery, which overcharges and swells the battery by boiling it dry).

A weak battery can be charged up on a battery charger, but if it became weak on its own it would be wise to replace it.

For now, to get the car started, give it a boost. (Refer to the "When to Jump-Start a Car and How" section on page 48.) Slow cranking can also be due to a faulty starter. This condition is known as starter drag, and it occurs when the starter motor components wear or burn out.

5. **One loud click each time the ignition key is turned.** This could indicate that the starter motor gear is trying to engage the flywheel but is not spinning it as it should. Rapping or banging on the side of the starter motor with a hammer while another person tries to start the car from inside sometimes works (for now). This indicates that the starter motor has a dead spot and needs to be replaced.

Caution: Always exercise extreme care when working around the engine!

A loud single click could also mean that the starter wants to turn or crank your engine but it cannot because the engine is seized or frozen stiff. This condition does not happen often, but if it does you are not going anywhere soon with your car.

6. **Grinding.** A grinding noise when starting indicates that the starter motor gear and flywheel gear aren't meshing smoothly for the starting process. The starter motor bolts and the starter may be loose and need to be tightened, or the starter motor gear may be worn or broken. The flywheel teeth may be worn or chipped or the flywheel cracked. In any of the above cases, a professional will have to do the necessary repairs.

WHEN TO JUMP-START A CAR AND HOW

Caution: Batteries can explode and battery acid can burn skin, eyes, and clothing. If battery acid contacts your eyes or skin, immediately flush the area with lots of water.

A person would jump-start his car when it will not start due to a dead or weak battery. To determine a dead or weak battery please refer to the "Starting Problems" section on page 43 for specifics. Basically, if your engine cranks (turns) slowly, clicks rapidly (when trying to start), shows signs of the lights being dim, or has no lights at all, give it a boost.

Note: If your car initially had full cranking power but did not start after multiple tries, then boosting probably will not help.

Each end of a booster cable consists of two clamps, a positive (red) and a negative (black). First, start the car that is giving the boost. Then connect a positive (red) clamp to the positive battery post (marked "pos" or "+") on the boosting (car running) battery. Next, connect the positive clamp on the other end of the booster cable to the positive post on the dead battery. Then go back to the other end of the cable and connect the black (negative) clamp to the "neg" or "−" post on the boosting battery. Finally, connect the other negative clamp to any exposed heavy metal part such as a nut or bolt in the engine compartment of the car with the dead battery.

Warning: Do not allow the cable ends to touch each other during the boosting procedure.

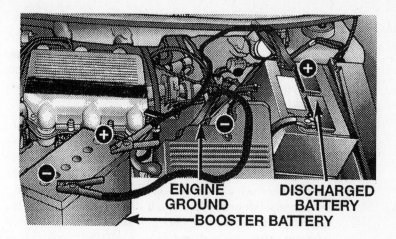

ENGINE GROUND   **DISCHARGED BATTERY**

←——**BOOSTER BATTERY**

Caution: Before making the last connection, "graze" the booster cable end over the last connecting point before you actually clamp it on. While doing so, you should see a slight sparking. If it should make a loud snapping sound together with a bright spark, do not connect it, and double-check your connections. Criss-crossing booster cables could cause your battery to explode. You could also melt wiring and even damage your onboard computer.

After all the connections are made, allow the running vehicle as much time as possible to recharge the dead battery. Then try to start the dead vehicle. Once it starts, disconnect the booster cables and have the battery and charging system checked by a professional.

Keeping a battery pack (a portable boosting battery) on hand in your home or trunk may prove to be invaluable. It makes for a quick, simple boost, especially when your battery goes dead at an inopportune time or place, and it has the advantage of allowing you to boost your car without the use of another vehicle and in places that would make it difficult or impossible to pull a vehicle next to yours.

Steering

Steering you in the right direction is the most important feature of your vehicle besides braking. The total loss of steering is not very common, but it does occur, usually as a result of driver neglect or a mechanic's error.

However, the normal wear and tear on your vehicle's steering system can loosen up the components, causing excessive play in the steering linkage. This will make your steering wheel less responsive and will also cause your tires to steer out of sync with one another. Such a condition will cause your tires to wear out prematurely, but more important, it will compromise your vehicle's ability to handle and steer precisely. Ultimately, severely worn-out parts such as tie rod ends or ball joints could disconnect from themselves, causing a total loss of steering.

Steering components are checked as part of your vehicle's state inspection but should also be inspected twice a year, especially under bumpy road conditions. What exactly should be checked?

1. **Tie rod ends.** Tie rod ends are adjustable components of the steering system. They are threaded on one end and can be shortened or lengthened by a mechanic during a wheel alignment in order to adjust the toe-in and toe-out of your vehicle's wheel direction. The other end consists of a studded ball in a socket, an assembly that enables this part to rotate as you steer the vehicle. This connection between the steering linkage and the wheel's spindle must be able to pivot as the car goes over bumps. There is a great deal of friction in the ball and socket. Years ago tie rod ends required grease to clean and lubricate them, but most modern vehicles employ low-friction tie rod ends. They use a highly polished ball stud encased in a rugged polymer bearing. They are pre-lubed and sealed at the factory and require no additional lubrication. This design reduces friction by two-thirds from the old type. These types of tie rod ends are built to a ten-year, 150,000-mile durability standard. Because of this improvement, tie rod ends are not

replaced as often as they once were. If you do need to change them, make sure your mechanic uses "low friction" replacement parts.

How will you know when they need to be replaced? Either your mechanic or wheel alignment technician will show you that the rubber boot of the tie rod end is cracked (allowing water and other contaminants in), or that the tie rod end is loose or has excessive end play. Any lateral free movement or up-and-down free movement between the ball and socket is unacceptable, as is any knocking sound made by the tie rod end when pressure is applied by hand or with channel lock pliers. Severe play can lead to the dislocation of the tie rod end, which will result in a total loss of steering.

2. **Ball joints.** The ball joint is a ball stud in a socket or housing. Some cars have both upper and lower ball joints, some just lower. In either case the ball joint connects the steering knuckle to the control arm. This connection cannot be a solid rigid fit. It must be able to pivot to allow for suspension jounce and rebound. It must also be able to rotate to allow for the steering knuckle to turn in order to point the wheels in the desired direction.

There are two types of ball joints, categorized into what are known as "loaded" and "unloaded" types. Loaded ball joints carry the load or force of the vehicle's springs. The weight of the vehicle and its passengers forces the ball stud of the ball joint into the bearing's surface. This type of ball joint has tremendous forces working against it. Unloaded ball joints, also known as "follower" ball joints, do not bear the weight of the vehicle. Their purpose is to provide a second pivoting point for the steering knuckle.

How do we know when to replace our vehicle's ball joints? With unloaded ball joints, manufacturers allow no, or zero, play. This means that under no circumstances should there be any free movement between the ball stud and the socket. If your mechanic can show you any perceptible movement, the ball joint should be replaced. If any ball joint has a rip or gouge in the dust boot, it is or will become contaminated with dirt and rust and should be replaced. A ball joint that is binding inside usually will make a creaking noise, sometimes accompanied by a vibration. This will need replacement.

Loaded ball joints usually wear out faster than unloaded ones. Some come with built-in wear indicators that make it easy to spot a worn-out part. Others need to be checked for two types of movement: axial movement, which is the vertical movement of the ball stud in relationship to the ball housing, and radial movement, which is side-to-side movement of the ball stud in its socket. Both movements need to be checked with a dial indicator and its readings compared to the manufacturer's tolerance. Most mechanics, however, will not take the time to set up a dial indicator. They will take the load off the ball joint by using a floor jack and use a pry bar to lift under the tire. A second mechanic will closely watch the ball joint during this procedure and determine if there is a lot of play. A minimal amount of play is acceptable; some ball joints are intentionally manufactured that way.

3. **Idler arm.** An idler arm is a device that guides the steering linkage smoothly during turns. When it wears out it gives slack to the steering linkage by moving up and down and not horizontally. This play causes the right wheel to work out of sync with the left. Your mechanic would be able to show you this excessive play in the idler arm by pressing up against it with a pry bar.

4. **Pitman arm.** The pitman arm is connected to the steering box, and its function is to push and pull the steering linkage during turning. It has a ball-and-socket system similar to that of a ball joint. When the ball socket wears down due to friction and contamination, excessive play sets in. This must be replaced when that happens.

5. **Centerlink.** The centerlink is a rod that connects the left side of the steering linkage to the right. It too has a ball-and-socket assembly on each end that requires replacement when it becomes worn down and develops free play.

6. **Sway bar links.** Sway bar links are located at each end of the sway bar. The purpose of the sway bar is to minimize body roll. Sway bar links connect the sway bar to the frame of the car or the strut. They consist of small rubber bushings or tie rod end ball studs. These links bear a lot of stress, especially in hard cornering. They tend to wear or break, causing a rattling noise.

7. **Rack and pinion.** Most cars today utilize a rack-and-pinion steering system. The rack consists of a flat slab of steel with teeth carved out of it. A pinion gear, which is connected to the car's steering wheel through the steering column, rolls against the rack as you steer your vehicle, causing the rack to move from side to side. This movement points the wheels in the desired direction.

Rack-and-pinion units work in conjunction with power steering pumps. These pumps pressurize fluid, making steering easier for the driver. Some cars use a variable-assist power steering system. This varies the amount of steering effort according to the speed of the vehicle. For parking maneuvers, maximum assist will be employed, while minimum assist is needed at highway speeds. The latter will improve steering stability and road feel at high speeds.

Today's steering racks should last over 100,000 miles. Frequent turning and tight parking situations will reduce the estimated life. Power steering leaks from the rack will also reduce its working life.

If you find it necessary to replace either your rack and pinion, steering box, or power steering pump, use this opportunity to flush out your power steering fluid and to replace it. If this is being done, make sure your mechanic removes all the air from the power steering fluid before you pick up your car. Otherwise the system will "whine" unnecessarily.

Struts and Shock Absorbers

What do struts and shock absorbers do? When do we need to replace them?

First off, let's explain the difference between a shock absorber and a strut. A shock absorber is an independent part that works in conjunction with the existing suspension system, while a strut is an integral part of the suspension system. Both struts and shocks control body motion and dampen wheel movement.

Basically, when your car drives over bumps or dips in the road or when you accelerate or stop quickly or change lanes abruptly, the body of the car reacts to inertia. The shocks and struts absorb these forces, allowing the body of the car to react to them with a limited or cushioned allowance. This controlled allowance prevents the tires from bouncing over bumps and prevents the body of the car from rebounding too quickly. Imagine that your tires are like basketballs being dribbled down the street. The strut or shock restricts the amount of bounce, keeping the tire from spending any unnecessary time away from the pavement. It also prevents the car from bottoming out over severe bumps or dips.

Shocks and struts are very important to the overall ride of the vehicle. Your car will handle better and stop over shorter distances when your shocks and struts are performing properly, and your tires will adhere to the road better over bumps and dips. Good shocks and struts will limit your vehicle from excessive nosediving during short stops. They will also help prevent your ABS brake system from engaging prematurely.

Shocks and struts are filled with either oil or a compressed gas. If the oil or gas seeps out, the shock or strut becomes soft and it loses its ability to work properly. If you notice a change in the way your car rides, especially over bumps, check your shocks. This change may be gradual and thus hard to detect.

Another telltale sign is if your tire or tires develop flat spots or cupping on the treads. This could be an indication that the tires are bouncing over bumps in the road.

A knocking noise over bumps or dips may be an indication that the strut or shock is broken either internally or at one of the mounting points.

Oil dripping down the cartridge of the shock or strut is a clear indication that the shock is in need of replacement.

Strut towers (mounts) sometimes have to be replaced along with the strut. This is where the strut mounts at the top to the body of the car. Have your mechanic check these when checking your struts.

When replacing your struts or shocks, look for a name-brand nitrogen gas shock, preferably with a lifetime guarantee. High-pressure shocks will give a stiffer ride, while low-pressure shocks will give a softer ride. Shocks and struts should not be changed to raise or lower the height of the vehicle. This is the job of the springs.

Insider's Tip

Springs support the vehicle's weight and in so doing affect the ride quality, ride height, wheel alignment, handling, and braking. All springs sag with age, as they typically support 600–1,300 pounds, this figure being multiplied over bumps. Some struts allow for a camber adjustment. Camber is one of the angles adjusted during a wheel alignment and is altered when you replace your struts. Consequently, you should get a wheel alignment done after these adjustable struts are changed. It is recommended to change all four struts or shocks as a matched set, although many car owners replace the front and rear sets independently.

Good shocks and struts prevent the body of the vehicle from compressing rapidly when stopping short and/or changing lanes suddenly, for instance to avoid an accident. This is especially important for SUVs that have a high center of gravity and are more prone to rollovers. Good, tight shocks and struts are very important to vehicles with ABS (antilock braking system). ABS prevents the tires from locking up, making it possible to steer under hard braking conditions. Turning hard and braking hard at the same time will cause the car to pitch to one side. A good strut or shock will minimize this pitch.

Timing Belt and Related Parts

Unfortunately, timing belts are one of the most overlooked maintenance-required components in your vehicle. Because they are not visible when you open up your hood, they fall into the category of "out of sight, out of mind." This oversight could result in a very serious and expensive engine repair. *Note:* Not all cars have timing belts. Some have timing chains, which require no maintenance.

The timing belt deteriorates over time. Heat from the engine hardens it and weakens its strands. In most cases the belt will look fine externally but may be on the verge of splitting internally. Deterioration is also accelerated if the belt gets soaked in oil leaking from a front engine seal.

The timing belt is one of the most crucial replacement parts of the engine. It should be replaced according to the manufacturer's maintenance schedule, which in most cases is at 60,000-mile intervals. The timing belt has in many but not all cases replaced the timing chain, which produces a noisier engine. It is rubber-based and has cogs or boxes built into it that match and drive (spin) the pulleys on the front of the engine. These pulleys, which are connected to the front of the crankshaft, the camshaft, and sometimes the water pump must be in perfect synchronization with one another at all times. Should this belt jump teeth or break, the engine will stall and on "interference engines" the pistons could collide with the valves, causing major damage to the engine. Non-interference engines will stall but not cause internal engine damage.

If your timing belt drives the water pump pulley, it is highly recommended that you replace the water pump at this juncture even if it is not faulty, because should the water pump fail at any later time, the new belt will jump out of sync and you will be back to square one or worse.

Along with the timing belt and water pump are tensioner pulleys. These pulleys or bearings spin and roll against the timing belt, keeping it taut at all times, not allowing it to get slack and jump teeth. As you can imagine, any parts that are constantly spinning at high speed and under pressure will eventually wear out and fail and should be replaced. Some engines have hydraulic tensioners that hydraulically put tension on the belt via a spinning bearing. This is a good time to change this also.

Finally, replacing the timing belt is an opportune time to replace the crankshaft seal, camshaft seal, and any other front engine seals, especially if the car is more than five years old. These seals prevent oil from leaking out of the front of the engine and onto the timing belt, which is made of rubber, causing the belt to disintegrate prematurely. Failure of the seals occurs when their rubber portion becomes hard due to age and extreme temperatures and can no longer seal the spinning shafts.

To summarize, the timing belt, water pump (if belt driven), tensioners, and seals should be replaced together because they are all crucial and related to one another. This job is labor-intensive, and to have to go back into this area of the engine at a later time would be a shame. I would also recommend to use OEM (original equipment manufacturer) parts for this job, especially for the water pump.

The outer belts—the belts that drive the alternator, A/C, and power steering pump—will have to be removed to replace the timing belt, so you may want to use this as an opportunity to replace them at no additional labor charge.

Tires and Wheels

Tires are a vehicle's reaction point to the road surface. They are the final link in the driver's chain of commands.

There are different circumstances that would make it necessary to replace your tires.

Mileage. Normal wear and tear on a tire wears down its tread. Sometimes this wear is uniform across the treads and sometimes it is not. In any event, it would be time to replace the tire if any tread depth was less than one-sixteenth of an inch. The "dime rule" can be used to make this measurement. Place a dime in the groove of the most worn-down tread, with FDR's head pointed toward the tire. Look from the side to see if the top of the head is visible. If it is, the tread of the tire has worn down past its limit and the tire cannot perform effectively on both dry and wet surfaces. In rain, the ability to disperse water away from the tire will be compromised and hydroplaning (when the tire loses contact with the road surface and skims over the water) will occur.

Tread wear indicators (bars) are constructed into the tread of the tires. These eight bars of rubber are evenly spaced every 45 degrees around the circumference of your tire. When you notice a solid patch across the tread of your tire in a few locations, your tire has worn out to the point that it should be replaced.

If the cords of the tire are showing, replace the tire immediately, as this condition can lead to a blowout.

Sidewall bulge (bubble). Bulges in the sidewall of a tire are a result of a torn belt in the tire's construction, usually due to a severe pothole or hitting a curb. They occur when your wheel goes into a pothole and the tire's walls are compressed between the pothole and the rim. This impact pinches the sidewall, causing it to tear, and the air pressure in the tire pushes outward, creating a bulge similar to an aneurysm. Bulging sidewalls can lead to blowouts, so replace the tire.

Insider's Tip

When checking the condition of your tires always check the inside tire wall, as sidewall bulges can occur on either sidewall of the tire.

Cupping or flat spots. When your tires' treads begin to look like the wheels on the Flintstones' car, they should be replaced. Cupping or flat spots occur when the tire bounces excessively, usually due to faulty shocks or struts. Parking the car in one spot for an extended amount of time can also cause flat spots. Whenever the tire's tread surface becomes uneven and not true to round, replace the tire.

Warping. Warping of the tire occurs when its inner belts shift or bend. A rolling tire will wobble, causing the steering wheel to wobble back and forth, especially at slow speeds.

Dry rot. Dry rot occurs when the rubber of the tire dries out due to age and the elements. When cracks become visible on either side of the tire, it is time to replace it.

Gouges. Every time you parallel park, you run the risk of scraping or gouging your tire's sidewall. Minor scrapes will not compromise the integrity of your tire, but deep tears or gouges will.

What you should know when you buy new tires:

High-performance tires. Some vehicles come standard with these. Like all tires, they come identified with a speed rating letter ranging from G (56 mph) to Z (149+ mph). Be sure to replace your tire with the proper speed-rated tire. You can, however, upgrade to a higher speed rating. The higher the speed rating, the better that tire can handle high speed and high heat conditions.

Low-profile tires. These have sidewalls that are short in comparison to the width of the tire. A tire that has a size of 225/40/16 has a sidewall that is only 40 percent of the width of the tire. They fit on wheels that are larger in diameter and so a low-profile tire is needed to accommodate for the oversize wheel. One would purchase low-profile tires because they have better handling around sharp turns since they bounce less, and because many people prefer the look of larger than stock (original) wheels. The downside of low-profile tires is that they give a harsher ride and offer less protection to the rim from potholes, making not only the rim more vulnerable to bending but themselves more susceptible to bulges. Also, they do not perform well in the snow.

Blems. Blemished tires perform and last as well as regular ones. They may have a cosmetic imperfection such as the letters on the sidewalls being upside down. You will be able to save money on these types of tires.

If you need to replace only two tires, try to match them exactly to the ones that are not being replaced. The next-best alternative is to match the tread pattern. Always put the better tires in the front (on front-wheel-drive cars), and never put two different-size tires on the same axle!

When buying new tires, ask about the manufacturer's warranty. What does it cover? How long does it take to get a refund if a defective tire needs to be replaced? How do they prorate the tire, and do they offer a goodwill adjustment if their tire is damaged by a road hazard? Ask which brand has the best warranty. Know that plugging a tire instead of patching it will void the warranty, so if it gets bitten by a nail, have it patched from the inside. Also, if you drive on a flat tire, even just for a short distance, you will destroy the tire and it will void the warranty.

To get the most out of new tires, check them periodically for the correct air pressure (check when the tires are cool) and have your wheels aligned once a year. This alignment will provide you with a complete front-end and suspension check, as a wheel alignment is worthless if your car's suspension has a problem.

FACTS ABOUT TIRES

➤ Underinflated tires—outer treads wear out faster, increase fuel consumption, create excessive heat, do not handle well.

➤ Overinflated tires—blow out easier, wear out faster, bounce or dribble.

➤ Tires should be patched, not plugged, for a longer-lasting repair.

➤ Nails in the sidewalls cannot be fixed safely with a patch. Play it safe and replace the tire.

➤ The softer the tire's composition, the better it will stick to the road, but it will wear down quicker.

➤ Tire rot is due to ozone, salt, and sun.

TIRE ROTATION

Tire rotation should be performed every 6,000–9,000 miles in order to extend the life of the tires. Front tires tend to wear out faster because, in addition to spinning, they also turn when steering and usually are under the weight of the engine. Rotating the front tires to the back will slow down their wearing-out process and allow the fresher tires to catch up.

Insider's Tip

Some high-performance tires are directional and should not be crossed to the other side of the car. These tires have an arrow that indicates the proper direction of tire rotation. Also, some vehicles have larger tires in the rear that cannot be rotated to the front.

Scam Alert

Place a dot of Wite-Out on your rear tires near the valve stem before you have the tires rotated. The dots, of course, should be found on the front tires of the car after they are rotated. This is a good way to see if you are really getting what you are paying for.

CHANGING A FLAT TIRE (JACKING UP)

The thought of changing a flat tire sounds simple to some and frightening to others. In reality it is a simple process but can be *very dangerous* if not done carefully. Always refer to your owner's manual and manufacturer's instructions and follow them carefully.

Caution: Never change your tire in a place that puts you in peril from moving vehicles. If you are on a highway, pull as far away from traffic as possible and put your emergency flashers on. If you are carrying a road flare, light it and place it well in advance of your vehicle.

First of all, check to see if the tire may have gone flat due to a slow leak. To check for this you will need a compact portable compressor or a can of Fix-A-Flat. You will need to fill your tire with air and see if it holds it. If it does, drive to a tire shop and have it permanently repaired. If it does not hold air, you will have no choice but to put your spare tire on.

Before doing anything else, check the spare tire to make sure it is holding air pressure. Press firmly on the tire to see if it is hard or use a tire gauge before you go through any steps needlessly.

Basic Steps for Changing a Flat Tire*

1. The car should be jacked up only on level ground with the emergency brake engaged and with a wheel chocked in front and behind. The point of this is to prevent the car from tipping over while it is jacked up.

2. Remove the spare tire from the car.

3. Remove the hubcap, if applicable, with a screwdriver or tire iron. Before you raise the car, crack or loosen the wheel (lug) nuts just one or two turns counterclockwise.

4. Secure the jack in the proper location under your vehicle as per the directions in your owner's manual and slowly jack up the car to the point where the spare tire will be completely off the ground. (Keep in mind that the spare tire with air in it needs more clearance to the ground than the flat one.) Make sure the jack is set properly so that the car is not rolling forward or backward and that the tire iron (if one is being used) is far enough away from your face should it snap back up at you.

5. Remove the lug nuts and pull the flat tire off the car. Place it on its side and push it halfway under the side of the car. That way, if the car were to fall off the jack it

---

* If your car is equipped with automatic air suspension (some Lincoln and Ford models), turn the air compressor switch (located in the trunk) to the off position before you jack up the car. Remember to turn it back on when you are finished.

would land on the tire and not on the ground. This could save body parts, and it's easier to re-jack the car up if it's not resting on the ground.

6. Put the spare tire on the car, face out, and spin the nuts or studs on, one by one, by hand clockwise to tighten. (*Note:* Lug nuts have tapered ends that center the rim to the car's hub. This tapered end faces the wheel.) Tighten them with your lug wrench but do not exert too much pressure on them until the car is lowered off the jack. After lowering, tighten completely and replace the hubcap, allowing for it to fit over the protruding tire valve.

7. When the job is complete, slowly test-drive the car and make sure it does not wobble or make any strange noises.

Caution: When you are finished replacing the tire, always secure heavy objects like the jack or wrench that could be propelled forward in the event of an accident.

WHEEL ALIGNMENT

Alignment of your wheels is essential for proper handling of your vehicle. Good tires that are properly aligned will prevent your car from pulling to one side or the other and will keep them adhered to the road, especially while rounding corners. Proper alignment will prevent your tires from wearing out prematurely and your car will get better fuel mileage and the tires will last much longer.

Some indications that your car's alignment is out of whack are: The tires screech around turns, the car pulls to one side or the other, or the tire surface is wearing unevenly.

Misalignment can be caused by a severe impact to the suspension, which can cause a bend or "play" in one of the many steering components. Certainly if you notice that your car handles or feels differently after banging through a pothole or hitting a curb or median, it would be important to check the car on an alignment machine, not just to see if it is out of alignment but to see what was damaged and how to remedy the problem.

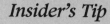

Insider's Tip

Sometimes a car pulls to one side on level ground because one of the front tires has developed a tread pattern that is off center. Switching the positions of your front tires can sometimes straighten out the problem. If the car pulls in the other direction after this operation, try mounting your front tires to the back.

Another cause of improperly aligned wheels could be due to worn-out front-end (and in some cases rear-end) suspension parts. Some of these parts are the tie rod ends, centerlink, idler arm, pitman arm, rack and pinion, ball joints, and bushings. They are discussed in more detail in the "Steering" section on page 50. If any one of these parts becomes worn out or damaged, it can knock the alignment out of whack and in some cases create a dangerous situation in which you might lose control of the vehicle. Once the front end is repaired and is "tight," a wheel alignment can be performed.

Scam Alert

Most cars can only be aligned in the front, so do not pay for a four-wheel alignment if the rear has no adjustment. The computer screen on the alignment machine will indicate if it is a two- or four-wheel alignment. However, the rear wheels are a factor in aligning the front wheels. They must be straight; otherwise the car will dog-leg in the rear.

WHEEL BALANCE

Wheels that are out of balance will cause the steering wheel to shimmy back and forth at speeds of approximately 60 mph. Sometimes an overall vibration in the car accompanies the shimmy.

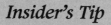

Insider's Tip

If your car pulls to one side on a level road, check to see that your tires have equal and proper tire pressure. The correct tire pressure can be found on a sticker that is either in the glove box or in one of the doorjambs.

What causes this? Tires and wheels may look perfectly symmetrical but can be heavier on one side than the other. When they spin rapidly, this imbalance of weight distribution causes the wheel and tire to vibrate.

To correct this problem, tires should be speed-balanced on a computerized, calibrated balancing machine when a tire is purchased, or when shimmying develops. To balance the tire, small weights are added to the wheel to compensate for the heavier side of the tire and wheel, thereby balancing it on its axis.

If the steering wheel slowly rocks back and forth at very slow speeds, this would indicate that either a wheel (rim) is bent or that the belt in the tire is bent. To locate the damaged tire, put the car on a lift and spin each tire individually and visually look for a wobble in the tire and/or wheel.

WHEEL (HUB) BEARINGS

Wheel bearings are an important component of your vehicle. They carry the weight of your entire vehicle and its occupants. This weight is increased due to inertia when stopping and turning.

The function of wheel bearings is to permit your wheels to roll smoothly and quietly under the weight of your vehicle. A humming noise is the major indicator of faulty wheel bearings—specifically, a humming noise that gets progressively louder the faster you go. This noise will change in sound when you turn the steering wheel slightly but quickly back and forth. Pinpointing which side the bad bearing is on might be difficult, because the sound that is created usually reverberates from the front of the vehicle. Checking which hub bearing is bad on the lift is usually impossible as it is a sealed unit into which one cannot see. Your mechanic can try to find the faulty bearing by putting the car into gear to allow the wheels to spin with the vehicle on the lift in hopes of hearing which wheel is humming, but unfortunately these bearings will not always make noise unless the weight of the vehicle is on them. On front-wheel-drive cars your mechanic could prevent one wheel or the other from spinning, allowing him to listen and compare sounds independently.

Insider's Tip

A tire that has a belt or tread problem will also make a humming sound that will get progressively louder with speed. If you experience this noise from the front of your vehicle, check your front tires before you replace an expensive hub bearing. If the tires look good, rotate them anyway to the rear and see if the humming noise follows them to the rear of the car. If this is the case, replace the faulty tire and save money on replacing the hub bearings.

If the faulty front-wheel-drive hub bearing cannot be pinpointed to one side or the other, you have two options. Replace one side, then test-drive the car. If the noise is gone it's your lucky day. So play lotto. If the noise is still there, replace the other side and consider that both bearings have had the same amount of wear and tear on them and the good one would become a bad one shortly thereafter anyway.

Another point to consider is that a hub or wheel bearing can be damaged from severe impact. This would come as a result of sliding sideways into a curb or median, or from a severe pothole that causes the rim to bend on impact.

Rear-wheel-drive vehicles have tapered roller bearings in the front. These are serviceable and do require adjustment and regreasing. Every time your vehicle is on the lift for an oil change the technician should spin the front wheels and also check to see that the bearings do not have free play. This is easily done by tak-

Tips Tips
Tips
ips T
Tip

Insider's Tip

Hub bearings that are wearing out from normal wear and tear create louder noise gradually, not abruptly. You might not notice this subtle change, whereas someone else who never drives in your car might notice that the car sounds loud at speed.

ing the bottom of the tire with your hands and pushing inward and then outward. If the wheel has any movement from this pushing or pulling, the bearing will need to be inspected and repacked with grease. The inspection would detect if the roller bearings, which are cylindrical rollers, have any imperfections in them, such as pitting or heat discoloration. If they do, replace them together with their matching race, which is the round metal part that the roller bearings roll against. If they do not show signs of damage, have them repacked with high-temperature bearing grease. After they are reinstalled and adjusted, the wheels should spin freely and smoothly without any side-to-side play. A bearing cap, which protects the bearings from the elements, should be cleaned and packed with fresh grease. Let's roll!

Transmissions

AUTOMATIC TRANSMISSIONS

The transmission is the "go-between" mechanism connecting the engine and the tires. Once the engine is started, it spins very fast. If it were connected directly to the wheels, they would spin whenever the engine was running. That would not be good.

Automatic transmissions use torque converters to engage the engine to the transmission. These take the place of the clutch system found on manual transmissions.

Aside from connecting the engine to the drive wheels, transmissions have speeds, or gears, that shift depending on the speed of the vehicle and the load or demand of the driving situation. Shifting between gears is a necessary function of the transmission.

On late-model vehicles most of the functions of the transmission, including shifting, are controlled by a computer system in conjunction with electrical switches and solenoids.

The most common transmission problems are:

➤ Your car does not move when you put it into drive or reverse

➤ It takes a few seconds before it engages into gear

➤ It shifts too late or too early

➤ It shifts with a noise or it bangs into the next gear

➤ It makes strange noises

➤ It shifts with a delay between gears

First, check the transmission fluid level. Check the level when the fluid is hot and the engine is idling with the vehicle on level ground and the transmission in park.

The transmission fluid should be pink, clear, and should not smell burnt—it should smell close to how it smells when it is still in its container. If it smells burnt and looks dark or brown, it should be replaced.

Insider's Tip

Transmission fluid should be replaced according to your vehicle maintenance schedule. Do not exceed 40,000 miles unless your newer vehicle's transmission fluid is not recommended ever to be changed. This is because some newer vehicles use "synthetic" transmission fluid. In such cases, the fluid, filter, and transmission pan gasket should all be replaced together. A kit, which includes the filter and gasket, is available from any auto parts store, or your repair establishment will provide one.

Note: On some vehicles, it has happened that the transmission will not engage with the new, clean transmission fluid. If this occurs, the new fluid will have to be replaced again with the original fluid.

If the transmission dipstick (not motor oil) reads low, add the appropriate amount, being careful not to overfill the unit. Follow the "Hot" and "Cold" marks on the dipstick if applicable.

Test-drive the car after you have leveled off the transmission fluid. If it still has one of the symptoms outlined above, a qualified transmission technician should analyze the problem. Get a few independent opinions and prices before picking the transmission shop. Ask what their guarantee policy is. Inquire if they can give you a loaner car while the job is being done, and if their guarantee will cover towing if your rebuilt transmission gives out while under warranty.

Insider's Tip

If your car, whether it has a manual or automatic transmission, does not engage in forward or reverse, the problem may not be the transmission at all. Axles that are connected to the transmission sometimes pop out from the case, giving the impression that the transmission is not working. To check this, the car must be on a lift and be checked visually to ensure that the inner axles are securely connected to the final drive.

Insider's Tip

Whenever a guarantee is offered, inquire about its length and if it covers parts *and* labor. Some guarantees are offered on parts only.

Many transmission shops advertise low prices. These ads may also say in fine print, "For most cars" or "Installation extra." Ask to see the last ten invoices that were repaired at their advertised low price. Transmission shops maximize their profits by selling transmissions, not small repairs on transmissions. If you agree to have your transmission rebuilt and agree on a price, make sure you put it in writing, and that the price is firm and will not increase upon any discoveries once the transmission is taken apart. Also establish if the torque converter, which is like a clutch for automatic transmissions, is included in the price. It is advisable to replace the torque converter when the transmission is being replaced.

On the rear of your engine is a crankshaft seal. Replacing this seal when the transmission is out of the car is relatively easy and inexpensive. You may want to take advantage of an opportunity to replace this seal, especially if your engine has over 75,000 miles or is over six years old.

Insider's Tip

A blown fuse can cause symptoms of a serious transmission problem.

MANUAL TRANSMISSIONS AND CLUTCHES

Manual transmissions (also known as "standard") are much simpler in design than automatics and in turn are much easier to diagnose for malfunctions.

Aside from connecting the engine to the drive wheels, manual transmissions have speeds or gears that need to be changed through shifting, at different intervals.

Here is a list of problems that can arise from a manual transmission or clutch:

➤ Slipping—the transmission is in gear but the car does not move, or it does move but the engine is revving faster than it should.

➤ Chattering—uneven engagement of the clutch.

➤ A grinding noise when shifting from one gear to another.

➤ Popping out of gear while driving.

➤ Soft or no clutch pedal resistance.

➤ Noise from the transmission in neutral with the clutch pedal up.

➤ Noise from the transmission in neutral with the clutch pedal depressed.

➤ Vibration at highway speed.

➤ A whining or humming noise in any or all gears.

Causes of these symptoms:

Slipping. A slipping clutch is one of the more common symptoms experienced and is indicative of a worn-out clutch. The clutch's purpose is to smoothly engage the flywheel, which spins with the engine, to the gears of the transmission. When the clutch pressure plate or clutch disc wears out, the clutch will slip, disengaging the engine from the transmission.

Insider's Tip

Before you rush to replace your clutch, first check it for proper adjustment. One way to do this is to make sure that your clutch pedal has about one inch of free play at the top. This means the pedal should have free travel of about one inch before it meets with stiffer resistance. If you don't have this free play, have your mechanic adjust your clutch first, then see if it helps.

Chattering. If your clutch chatters on release or it does not feel smooth anymore, this could be an indicator that the clutch assembly is glazed or warped and needs replacement. In addition, the flywheel needs to be refaced at this time. This refacing is done by a lathe that cuts the face of the flywheel, leaving a true flat surface. In addition, a worn pilot bearing or bushing will cause chattering. Externally, a broken motor or transmission mount can also cause chattering.

Grinding gears. This can occur when the clutch pedal is not depressed all the way between shifts or if there is a problem with the clutch cable or clutch hydraulics. If the clutch system is working properly, the culprit is most likely the gear synchronizer. The synchro slows down the spinning gear, enabling two gears to smoothly mesh. If the synchro on a particular gear is shot, that gear will grind when shifting. Nothing short of a transmission rebuild will fix this.

Popping out of gear while driving. This indicates that either the shifter linkage needs to be adjusted or that an internal part such as a gear sleeve or fork needs replacement.

Soft or no clutch pedal resistance. If your car has a clutch cable, have it checked. If your car has a hydraulic clutch system, the clutch master cylinder and clutch slave cylinder must be checked. First off, check the clutch fluid level. If it's low, top it off and check for leaks under the clutch master and slave cylinders. Replace these as needed.

Noise from the transmission in neutral with the clutch pedal up. Have the transmission checked. It could be a bad input shaft bearing.

Noise from the transmission in neutral with the clutch pedal depressed. It could be that the clutch release bearing (throwout bearing) is shot. Have this checked.

Vibration at highway speed. This could be caused by a number of things. First have the driveshaft and universal joints checked. A bad axle or CV joint might be the culprit. Lastly, have all your tires speed-balanced.

A whining or humming noise in all gears. First make sure your manual transmission is filled with oil to its proper level. If it still whines, have it checked by a transmission shop.

Insider's Tip

Whenever the transmission is taken out of the car, it opens the opportunity to replace the engine's rear main seal and pilot bearing. If these two parts were to fail at a later date, the transmission would have to be removed again to access them.

Tune-ups

Tune-ups are almost becoming a thing of the past, especially when compared to older cars. Late-model cars no longer have ignition points and carburetors that require periodic maintenance. However, late-model cars do have spark plugs, air filters, PCV valves, and fuel filters, among other serviceable parts, that do need replacement when they get dirty or worn out.

The spark plugs tend to last much longer on late-model cars because the engine is monitored by the onboard computer. The computer controls the air/fuel mixture and ignition timing. In turn, the engine runs cleaner and spark plugs last longer. If your vehicle uses platinum spark plugs, they can last as long as 100,000 miles.

The air filter catches dirt particles before they enter the air intake. Eventually it will clog and restrict air from entering the intake. You can either replace it once a year or take it out and visually inspect it.

The fuel filter on fuel-injected cars is encased in metal, therefore it cannot be checked internally. It is recommended that you replace the fuel filter every 25,000 miles.

Telltale signs of an engine in need of a tune-up are:

➤ Poor gas mileage

➤ Misfiring (engine does not run smoothly)

➤ Difficulty starting, especially on wet or humid days

➤ Sluggish acceleration

Any or all of these symptoms might be an indication of an engine in need of a simple tune-up. There are, however, many other variables that influence the engine's performance. These variables may need to be diagnosed through the use of a computerized diagnostic system. (Refer to the "Check Engine Lights/Codes" section on page 24.)

If you experience a rough (coughing) sensation on acceleration, check the large rubber hose that connects the air flow meter to the intake manifold for a crack. When you accelerate, especially from a dead stop, your engine lifts just a bit. If there is a crack in this large intake hose, it will spread open, causing the engine to gulp air. This creates a coughing effect as the engine drops back to its normal resting place. Taping the crack with duct tape will temporarily fix the problem, but replace the hose as soon as possible.

Winterizing

Winterizing is a vague term that infers there must be some action taken for your car to perform and survive the winter. Is there?

Yes and no. Yes, because the engine coolant or antifreeze should be clean and effective. The antifreeze is a liquid that is pumped by the water pump through the engine block, where it absorbs the heat of the engine's combustion chambers, then into the radiator, where it cools down and returns back into the engine, and so on. Before antifreeze was created, water was used. The problem with water is that it freezes below 32 degrees Fahrenheit. Freezing water in an engine block or radiator expands and will crack the engine block or radiator. To remedy this, round metal plugs called freeze-out plugs are pressed into the water jacket of the engine and are designed to pop out if the coolant freezes, generally saving the engine from cracking. Antifreeze has a much lower freezing temperature that can both cool the engine and not freeze up when the engine is not running in a cold climate. "Potent" antifreeze is antifreeze that will not freeze at cold temperatures at all. You can easily check the strength of your antifreeze by testing a sample of it from your car's radiator (check it when the engine is cold) with an antifreeze tester. If it is weak, open the radiator petcock, usually located at the base of the radiator, and allow the weak antifreeze to drain out. Opening the radiator cap will vent the system and speed up the process. Starting the engine for thirty seconds will allow more antifreeze from the engine block to drain out. Remember to dispose of the old antifreeze according to local statutes. It is sweet to some animals and will kill them if ingested, so exercise caution.

There are different types of antifreeze on the market. Older cars use the conventional green antifreeze, while late-model cars use the maroon. The maroon antifreeze, known as extended life antifreeze, is advertised to protect your cooling system for five years or 100,000 miles. It can be added to your existing Dex-Cool (General Motors) antifreeze and is safe on aluminum or brass radiators. (Look for antifreeze that can last as long as fifteen years coming onto the market soon.) Antifreeze is sold either full-strength, which needs to be diluted with 50 percent water, or pre-mixed, which can be added directly into the radiator or radiator reservoir.

Insider's Tip

Insist that your mechanic use premium or name-brand antifreeze. There is inferior-quality, diluted, and even recycled antifreeze on the market that your mechanic could sell you to boost his profit margin.

Dirty or rusty antifreeze may still be effective in cooling the car and in not freezing, but rusty antifreeze should be changed before it damages gaskets, the water pump, the radiator, and the heater core. Just draining and replacing with fresh antifreeze will help, but it is best to flush the system with a chemical available in all auto parts stores. Follow the directions on the product. Having the radiator removed and boiled out if the antifreeze is very rusty is advisable.

At all times of the year, make sure that your belts and all coolant-related hoses are not about to blow. The cold of winter makes these hoses and belts much more brittle and susceptible to snapping. Check them for dry cracks, bulging, or if they are brittle. Brittle hoses may crack on inspection, so be prepared in this event. Check all fluids, including the windshield washer fluid. Check the wiper blades and replace them if they are streaking or brittle.

Replacing your thermostat every four or five years as a matter of preventative maintenance is a good idea. The thermostat is a small valve that when closed (when cold) blocks the flow of coolant to the radiator. This blockage allows the coolant to reach operating temperature at about 180 degrees Fahrenheit. Most engines are designed to operate efficiently at this temperature. Without the presence of a thermostat or if the thermostat was stuck in the open position, the engine would not reach its operating temperature and the car's heater would not blow very hot air. On the other hand, if the thermostat was jammed shut, the coolant would be blocked from entering the radiator and your car would quickly overheat.

Thermostats are relatively easy to replace, although they can be a problem if the housing bolts are rusted in. Because they are usually not very expensive to replace, let a professional do the job. An opportune time to replace the thermostat is when you are draining or flushing the engine.

Scam Alert

If you take your car in for a flush or thermostat change, make sure you wait and watch because it would be easy for a mechanic to tell you it was replaced when in fact it was not. Marking the thermostat bolt with a small dot of Wite-Out before the job and checking to see if it was untouched after the job will tell you if someone actually removed the bolt.

Note: Whenever flushing the antifreeze, keep the heater control to the "high heat" position to allow the heater core to be flushed in the process.

When You Need
to See a Mechanic:
How to Deal with Him

*W*ho fixes cars?

1. Dealerships

2. Chain stores

3. Franchises

4. Independents

5. Backyard mechanics

The Pros and Cons

1. **Dealerships** employ factory-trained mechanics and use OEM (original equipment manufacturer) replacement parts. These facilities generally use the latest diagnostic equipment, and the mechanics become familiar with the job at hand because they often repair the same model cars and encounter the same repairs.

All of this makes running this type of shop very expensive and consequently more expensive to the consumer. Dealerships do, however, have four sources of income—new car sales, used car sales, part sales, and service. These sources can help offset their overhead.

A drawback of dealerships is that a different mechanic will work on your car each time you bring it in unless you can make a request from the service manager.

2. **Chain stores** fix a variety of different car models and generally do a lot of volume. They tend to be less expensive than dealerships and usually stock a large selection of parts, which are usually under their own name brand. The repairs they do are usually the type that can get you in and out as soon as possible. They usually guarantee their work, and if they are large they might have branches at many locations.

On the downside, if the chain store offers its mechanics a piece of the action (commission) for selling the work, the mechanics might be overanxious to sell you work you really do not need.

These types of shops generally will not assign the same technician to your car each time.

3. **Franchise muffler shops or transmission shops** are owned and operated by individuals. The advantage to these types of shops is that you receive the benefits of both a large company's resources and an individual owner's interests. These shops are usually well stocked and managed. They benefit from large-scale advertising and they usually offer good guarantees.

Because muffler shops and transmission shops primarily repair mufflers and transmissions, they have more experience and equipment in these fields than general repair shops.

The downside is that they do not use OEM parts and the consumer pays for their aggressive advertising.

4. **Independent shops** rely on word-of-mouth referrals or local advertising. They are owned by individual proprietors or partnerships. They may be small or large, but generally they offer a more personalized service. You may come to know the owner or one of the mechanics on a first-name basis. (Remember, it is harder to take advantage of a repeat customer, especially if you develop a rapport with them.) Independent shops are usually much cheaper than dealerships and, depending on the individual proprietor, can offer professional and honest service. Another advantage is that the cost of repairs may not always be set in stone. If business is slow or if the repairs are extensive, an independent shop manager may cut a deal to secure the job.

The downside is that an independent shop may not have the expertise of a dealership on some specific models and repairs. After all, someone who fixes the same type of automobile day in and day out might have the edge over a mechanic who develops his work experience over many different models.

5. Due to zoning laws and perturbed neighbors, **backyard mechanics** are not as prevalent as they once were. However, some wage-earning mechanics do take side jobs to make extra money. The only real benefit is that a backyard mechanic can afford to charge you a lot less than a shop because he does not have the same overhead. The downside is that he probably does not have a lift, which is sometimes necessary to work efficiently. He does not have insurance in the event your car kills someone or catches on fire after it was improperly repaired. You may save some money on the repair but the risk in the event of a problem is high.

Finding the Right Shop

There are several key factors to finding the right shop:

➤ Look up cartalk.com on the Internet and find "Mechan-X-Files" (under the "Actual Car Information" tab) to read about other people's experiences with local mechanics and for ratings on their shops.

➤ Referrals: Use other people's experiences, both good and bad, to pick a shop that meets your criteria. And remember that the backbone of any shop lies in the competence of its staff and technicians.

➤ References: Ask the shop if you can contact two customers for references. Find a shop when you are not rushed, pressured, or panicked.

➤ Look for a neat, well-organized appearance.

➤ Look for a shop where you have someone to speak to who is courteous, helpful, and takes the time to listen and answer questions.

USING THE INTERNET AND MORE

Using the Internet to discover helpful information about auto-related problems can be illuminating.

The problem that you may be experiencing with your car may be inherent in your vehicle's specific model due to an engineering or manufacturing flaw. These problems, complaints, and remedies may be registered with the National Highway Traffic Safety Administration (www.nhtsa.dot.gov). Look in the "Defect Investigations" database. This information may prove to be invaluable in diagnosing and repairing your vehicle.

Another vital source for automobile technical information could be provided to your mechanic through an organization called the International Automotive Technicians' Network (iATN). The iATN offers you the combined knowledge of more than 48,000 industry professionals networking together. They also offer a Shop Finder that will help you locate the nearest shop in their network. Their Web site is at www.iatn.net. Your mechanic would have to register with them first before he could access information from them.

Look for trade school diplomas and certificates of advanced coursework. Depending on what part of the country you live in, you may or may not have choices of certified shops to consider when getting your vehicle repaired. And, as usual, the definition of "certified shop" certainly can vary from shop to shop and program to program. Here are a few you might find available in your area:

The Motorist Assurance Program (MAP). The mission of this program is to standardize vehicle inspections. In order to be certified by MAP, repair shops must adhere to the following regulations:

➤ They cannot perform work on any car without the written approval of the owner.

➤ They must be legally organized for at least six months prior to certification.

➤ None of the employees in the shop can have been convicted of offenses related to fraud in the marketplace for at least two years.

➤ They must use third-party mediation and/or arbitration to solve any disputes between the customer and the repair shop.

There are more than 4,000 shops affiliated with MAP. For more information about the organization, go to their Web site at www.motorist.org.

American Automobile Association (AAA). Probably one of the most well-known automobile associations in the country, AAA has been active since 1902. Their service specialists inspect repair facilities for appearance, equipment, existence of ongoing training programs, community reputation, cleanliness, and the competency of the mechanics. AAA-approved repair shops guarantee their work for a minimum of twelve months or 12,000 miles, whichever comes first. In the case of a dispute between the customer and the shop, the shop will adhere to AAA's judgment. Their Web site, at www.aaa.com, contains detailed information about the organization and will help you find certified shops in your area.

ALLDATA—CAIS. ALLDATA is a leading provider of electronic automotive diagnostic and repair products and information to repair shops. To make sure that technicians know about all ALLDATA products and tests, they have developed CAIS (Certified ALLDATA Information Specialist) certification. CAIS exams are structured to ensure that technicians not only develop expertise with the systems they have studied but that they are also on the cutting edge of automotive repair technology. When 75 percent of a shop's technicians attain CAIS certification, it becomes a CAIS Certified Shop. You can find local shops—as well as other information—on their Web site at www.alldata.com.

Automotive Service Association (ASA). The ASA is a not-for-profit trade association that boasts 12,000 members. Founded in 1951, ASA is an organization for managers and owners of repair shops who are committed to delivering quality repairs and service to their customers. Shops associated with ASA are identified by the red, white, and blue ASA sign. For more information, check out www.asashop.org.

ASE BLue Seal of Excellence. While most other organizations certify individual automotive service businesses, ASE (the National Institute for Automotive Service Excellence) is unique in that it recognizes individual technicians who meet its exacting standards. However, if 75 percent of the technicians working in a shop are ASE-certified and if at least one of those technicians is certified in each service area offered by the ASE, the shop will be officially recognized by ASE as a Blue Seal establishment. There are approximately 960 such shops in the country. For more information, log on to www.asebluesseal.org.

Program groups. Some organizations offer automotive repair shop programs and benefits to project a more professional image. Some include codes of ethics, technicians, warranties, and more. NAPA, CARQUEST (Tech-Net), Auto Pride, Parts Plus, Auto Value, and Bumper to Bumper are examples of these programs. For more information about each of them, visit their respective Web sites:

NAPA—www.napaonline.com

CARQUEST—www.techauto.com

Auto Pride—www.autopride.com

Auto Value—www.800autotalk.com

Parts Plus—www.partsplus.com

Bumper to Bumper—www.800autotalk.com

But don't assume that if a shop is *not* certified that you will be ripped off or get inferior service. There are plenty of non-certified shops that provide excellent service at reasonable costs. But knowing about these programs and associations gives you another tool to help you go out and find the best mechanic for you and your car.

How Can I Be of Help to My Mechanic in Pinpointing a Problem with My Car?

Sometimes problems develop in your vehicle that are not obvious even to a professional. Giving your mechanic some clues can aid him in finding out exactly what's wrong. Making a list as things develop can be helpful, because sometimes the problem miraculously goes away on its own as you approach your repair shop.

Here is a list of things to take notice of:

1. **Unusual sounds.** Notice when they occur:

➤ When the engine is running in park

➤ Only when the car is moving

➤ Only when the car is hot or when it is cold

➤ Only over bumps

➤ Only on acceleration

➤ Only when braking

➤ Only when turning

➤ Only when the transmission shifts

➤ Only at highway speed

➤ Weather-related—damp or raining

As funny as it may seem, try to mimic the kind of sound you hear, or if possible tape-record the sound if it only happens sporadically.

2. **Leaks.** If you have a drip under your car, lay a clean paper towel under the area where it drips to take to the repair shop as a sample.

3. **Odors.** Odors can lead your nose to overheating brakes or plastic stuck to your car's exhaust. The odor of gasoline should be taken more seriously. If you smell gasoline, check under your car and under your hood for a leak. Because of gasoline's

volatile nature you should seriously consider having your mechanic come to you to check it out, or have your car towed in. Follow your nose . . .

4. **Smoke.** Where there is smoke there is not always fire, but there is heat. Smoke coming from your tailpipe or from under your hood is an indication that something is wrong. It could be that your car is burning oil or antifreeze or your valve cover is leaking oil onto the exhaust manifold and burning off. In any event, have your vehicle checked out.

5. **Warning lights or gauges.** These give you an indication that something is not right. Refer to your owner's manual to determine what your vehicle is telling you and what you should be doing about it.

If any light should come on while the engine is running, it would be an indicator that a system in the vehicle is not functioning and a situation is developing. All of these lights will and should light up when you turn the key to the ignition mode just before starting the vehicle. This lets you know that the bulb for each warning light is functioning. All these lights will turn on in the event the vehicle stalls out, because this will put the vehicle back into the ignition mode.

If any warning light should come on while you're driving, or if a gauge indicates a reading out of the norm, refer to your owner's manual.

Warning: Do not continue to drive if the oil light comes on (especially if it is accompanied by a ticking or knocking from the engine or if the overheating light comes on). Severe engine damage could result from ignoring these lights or gauges. Remember: Yellow lights indicate caution; red lights indicate imminent problems or danger.

6. **Fuel economy.** Sudden drops in your gas mileage would indicate that your engine's efficiency has been compromised. There are many variables related to engine performance, so have your mechanic evaluate the problem.

7. **Engine performance/acceleration.** A drop in engine response or a shaky engine at idle should be checked out by your mechanic.

8. **Fluid levels.** If you need to add any fluids, especially regularly, you should ask yourself or your mechanic where the fluids are going.

9. **Loud, high-pitched screeching, especially when cold.** A loose fan belt will screech when cold, but the sound will usually subside as the belt heats up.

10. **Noise or sensation when braking.** Try to explain to your mechanic what you hear and when you hear it. Describe the sensation you feel on your brake pedal. Does it pulsate? Do you need to pump it up to get brake pedal pressure? Is it hard?

11. **Handling.** Does your car steer or handle poorly? Does it screech around turns or pull in one direction? It could need a wheel alignment or just air in its tires.

12. **Hard to start.** When it is wet out. Trouble starting or a rough-running engine on damp days can occur when the ignition wires or distributor cap have absorbed moisture. Replace them, or at least try to dry them off for a temporary fix. There is a spray-on product available at auto parts stores designed for this purpose.

No matter what kind of repair shop you choose, there are certain things you must do before taking your car in for a repair:

➤ Ask and call a few of the shop's customers for their comments.

➤ Call for an appointment if at all possible.

➤ Mark the parts to be replaced with a small dot of Wite-Out. Check for this dot after this part was supposedly replaced.

➤ Test-drive the car with your mechanic to point out what may be wrong with it.

➤ When you leave your car for a repair, take time to point out to the manager the aesthetic condition of the vehicle.

Recommend that they cover or tape sensitive areas around the repair to avoid damage to your car's finish. This will ensure that there will be no question as to a dent that was not there when you left it. Most shops will look over the car first. If they don't, you should. (You could follow the same advice when leaving your car in a parking lot.)

➤ Have a detailed list of what is happening. For example: noises, runs rough, stalls, noise over bumps, etc. Also note when it is happening. For example: when the car is cold, hot, when humid or raining.

➤ Do not diagnose the job yourself and give the go-ahead to repair it. If the repair shop repairs what you said was wrong, they will insist on payment even if your diagnosis was incorrect.

➤ Never leave anything of value, such as tapes, tokens, E-ZPass, illegal drugs, weapons, etc., in your car when you leave it for service.

➤ Fuses protect many of your vehicle's electrical systems. If a fuse blows, the system or equipment it was protecting will stop working. Always check to see if your fuse is blown. Look through the sight on the fuse to see if it is burnt out or use a light tester to check it.

➤ Always leave your phone numbers, your keys (take your personal or house keys with you), and wheel lock keys (if applicable).

➤ Cut out the middleman. If the job is being sent from one shop to, let's say, a body shop or glass shop, take it there directly and avoid paying the middleman's markup.

During the repair process:

➤ Do not rush or press a technician for an on-the-spot diagnosis or price quote. This can lead to a possible misunderstanding down the road. Give him a chance to diagnose the problem properly and to check the price of the parts and their availability and the required labor involved.

➤ Make every effort to be viewed as a good customer by your repair shop's staff. A good customer from a repair shop's viewpoint is one that does not call every hour and does not rush the work process. A good customer does not stand over the shoulder of the mechanic as he works. A good customer also recognizes that repairing a car can sometimes be met with complications. A good customer pays for the repairs at the time of their completion and personally thanks or tips the mechanic who repaired his car.

After the repair is done:

➤ Test-drive the car with your mechanic, if applicable, to see, hear, and feel that all is well.

➤ Carefully check your bill. See what you are paying for. Ask if any changes were made compared to the estimate and do the math to make sure it adds up correctly.

➤ Keep a log of all repairs. If a repair shop were to inform you that you need, for instance, a new set of struts, you can reflect back to your receipts to see if you have ever had them replaced, who replaced them, and if they are under warranty. You can also use these records to compare prices from one shop to another.

Why Do Some Mechanics Have Such Bad Reputations?

When I was growing up I was under the impression that large, established corporations were inherently legitimate. I believed that everything I read in the newspaper had to be 100 percent the truth. As I grew older I came to realize that all businesses are out to make money, as much as they possibly can. Well, many mechanics are the same way. They can take advantage of consumers by using the consumers' lack of knowledge to their advantage. This is further exacerbated when your vehicle breaks down at the most inopportune time or place.

Knowing whom you are dealing with is crucial. Understanding that every businessman wants to succeed is obvious. Finding an establishment that wants to earn its money legitimately is difficult.

There was a time not so long ago when a mechanic could legitimately find something wrong with your two-year-old car, especially if it was driven in stop-and-go situations. These days, the auto repair industry is faced with the challenge of finding legitimate work. This is due to a number of factors. First of all, vehicles are being built better and require less maintenance. Secondly, many vehicles are leased and subsequently are not as well cared for as vehicles that are operated by their owners. Lastly, when the economy is off, people do not spend money on their vehicles unless it becomes absolutely necessary.

A mechanic must have the ability to show and explain what is needed and why. A customer will have more confidence in the repair facility if they understand what is going on, as opposed to just seeing someone drive their car onto a lift in a customer-restricted area. Repairs such as brake pads, leaks, broken or worn belts, and loose front-end parts are obvious even to the layperson. To instill confidence, the mechanic must stay in touch with you and inform you if any additional repairs are needed.

The customer, by nature, wants to spend as little as possible on repairing and maintaining his or her vehicle. Simultaneously, customers want to have a complete and trustworthy repair. Not only do they want to spend as little money as possible, they also want to spend as little time as possible. They do not want to wait, and they do not want to bring back their car because the repair was not done properly.

Now, let us look at the other side. What problems do repair shops have to deal with? For starters, the labor force, parts availability, know-how for a vast range of repairs on different types of vehicles, the proper tools, paperwork, permits, oil disposal, waste disposal, overhead, new technology, and insurance claims.

Finding new customers is a challenge. Better-built cars, auto leasing, stiff competition, and location all affect business. A successful business cannot just depend on customers finding you. A successful business needs to reach out and bring new customers in through the use of advertising, promotions, and by satisfying their customers so that they can spread their positive experiences with their friends, family, and co-workers.

POSTED: DUE TO INSURANCE REGULATIONS, NO UNAUTHORIZED PERSONNEL BEYOND THIS POINT.

Is this really an insurance regulation aimed to prevent possible injury to customers, or is it a ploy to keep customers in the dark?

It is quite possible to be injured in and around an automobile repair shop. There are many hazards all around— oil on the floor, air hoses being moved, power tools being used, cars on lifts that can fall off. There truly is a real danger to the customer and a real liability to the shop in the event of an injury or death.

For this reason customers are forbidden from entering the repair shop. Simultaneously, this restriction also keeps customers from interfering with the technicians as they work. Unfortunately for the customer, she cannot benefit from watching the repair as it takes place. It puts her literally in the dark during the repair process. If this is your shop's policy, as a consumer you should demand to be escorted into the shop to see the necessary work before and after it is completed.

The Most Common Conflicts Between Mechanics and Customers

1. **Price changes.** Price increases can result from many legitimate causes. For instance, a shop looks up in a labor guidebook the labor hours required to replace a water pump. On this particular model car from 1995 through 2002 the guidebook allows for three hours to complete the job, and the shop will give you an estimate or a price quote accordingly. But a problem might arise, such as if one of the bolts holding the water pump on your vehicle snaps due to corrosion and fusion while the mechanic is trying to release it. Now this three-hour job turns

into a twelve-hour job because the engine has to be lifted out to access and remove the one broken bolt, due to no fault of the mechanic (as it would have been if he had overtightened [over-torqued] it on its installation). The bolt snapped because its integrity was compromised due to age and corrosion. This would not have happened on the same model car, same engine but on a newer vehicle.

The consumer needs to understand that his or her vehicle is a machine that is subject to many potential problems. Issues that present themselves during a repair can only be resolved through close communication and understanding. Consumers should not jump to the conclusion that they are being ripped off. If a situation changes, there must be a reason for the change, and you are entitled to an explanation that satisfies you.

Everything is negotiable. If discussing the situation leaves you and the repair shop at odds with each other, maybe a compromise can be reached. Splitting the difference between the estimated time and the actual time might leave both parties less offended.

2. **Not having the repair completed when promised.** "What? The car is not ready yet?" Your mechanic tells you the parts had to be ordered and they did not come in yet. What you should remember is that most shops want to repair and release your car as soon as possible. After all, the sooner you pick up your car the sooner they will get paid. Another factor is space and liability. Your car sitting on his lot takes up valuable space and is a constant liability for theft or damage.

However, cars are not always repaired in the order they come in. A shop manager may bump another car in front of yours for a variety of reasons. For instance, a quick, straightforward brake job might yield more profit than a heater core replacement that tends to be more involved and intricate.

A customer who rolls in for a job that needs to be done right away will take precedence over a customer who just drops off and leaves. The shop manager or owner does not want to see that walk-in customer go elsewhere for his repair. The car that was left unattended will just have to wait, since that job has already been secured.

Another reason your car may not be completed at the promised time is overbooking. Repair shops do not like to turn away work, so they book jobs even though they know they will not get to them as promised. They can always blame the delay on a part that was back-ordered or out of stock.

Insider's Tip

One way of dealing with a shop that is procrastinating on a repair is to wait. If you have young children or can borrow some (the more the merrier), wait with them. Be sure to dispense plenty of high-sugar soda and items that are sticky or crumbly. Crying babies and stinky diapers can accelerate a repair job tremendously. The shop owner will want to send you on your way as soon as humanly possible.

Another ploy used by mechanics is to start the job, take parts off your vehicle, and hold it hostage. This way if you do reach your boiling point and you demand that your vehicle be returned, you will have to pay a partial labor or diagnostic fee.

As frustrated as you may be, there is a risk involved with taking a job away from a mechanic in midstream. A disgruntled mechanic may sabotage the job or leave parts missing for the next poor soul that gets it.

If at some point shortly after you have left your vehicle for a repair and you change your mind, usually because you have investigated the situation further, do not call the shop on the telephone to cancel the order. If they are desperate for the job, they will tell you that their mechanic has already started on it even if he has not, and that there will be a serious charge involved for his time. With this, the shop manager will immediately put one of his men on the car to take as much apart as possible before you return to see for yourself. Instead, personally go back there unannounced and retrieve your vehicle before anyone has a chance to lay a finger on it. If you have a problem being direct as to why you are taking back your car, you can tell them that the expense of the repair will cost you your marriage or that your neighbor is a mechanic and offered to fix it for free.

3. **"You fixed my flat tire but now my radio does not work."** This is known in the industry as "Eversinceya complex" (Ever since ya fixed my car something else doesn't work.) I have seen and experienced many scenarios over the years that leave me believing that some customers are not ethical or rational. Here are just a few:

A gentleman once came in to have his electric window repaired. It went neither up nor down. The problem was in the power window motor, which I replaced, and sent him on his way. Two days later he returned complaining that his brakes squeaked and that he had never had this problem before his window motor was replaced. He insisted that I must have inadvertently screwed up his brakes. When I explained to him that one was not related to the other, he left angry, convinced that I somehow was responsible for his squeaky brakes.

Another gentleman brought in his car. We changed the oil, the brake pads, and the rotors, and gave it a tune-up and a new muffler. A month later he called to tell me that his transmission was slipping. I told him to take it to a transmission specialist for an evaluation of the transmission, as we did not repair transmissions. He became perturbed with this and complained to me that he would not have spent money on the other repairs with me if he had known that his transmission was going to break. For some reason he must have thought that I could predict the future with regard to his transmission. I explained to him that his list of things to do that was presented to me a month earlier did not reflect upon any transmission problems. I also reminded him that when he came to pick up his car we both test-drove it with no hint of any transmission problem. All of this was to no avail.

"It wasn't like this when I left my car . . ." I recently heard this when a customer complained that his steering wheel now had a wobble at slow speeds that he insisted was not there before we replaced his pitman arm (a steering component). I informed him that the pitman arm was replaced properly and that it was physically impossible to have been installed improperly, as the part has grooved splines that fit one way and one way only. After test-driving his car I felt the wobble and determined that one of his front tires was warped. I switched his front tire for the back one and the problem was identified. It was obvious to me that the problem had been there all along but the owner may not have noticed it.

In any event, both parties have to work to find a mutually acceptable settlement in resolving issues. Always try to keep an open mind and an open channel to communicate with your shop. If all else fails, getting louder might work.

Through my experiences with the public I have found that people who are logical are also open-minded. An open-minded person, as suspicious as they may be as a consumer, will see things for what they truly are.

Occasionally a repair may have an adverse affect on another part of the vehicle. Sometimes it may be related, sometimes not. Having a repair performed on your car may legitimately create other problems. For instance:

➤ Removing other parts to access the repair compromises them or subjects them to possible damage.

➤ Leaning into an engine compartment can damage or disconnect delicate parts.

➤ Using a torch to cut, weld, or heat parts may melt or damage parts.

➤ Using the wrong tool may strip or damage bolts, screws, or parts.

➤ Disconnecting the car's battery, which is necessary to perform some repairs, will cause the clock and radio functions to be reset. On some anti-theft radios, a code must be reprogrammed into the unit for it to function again. Consider that on older vehicles the clock may never restart.

➤ Disconnecting any of the emission components will cause the check engine light (MIL) to illuminate.

➤ Working with sharp, heavy metal tools on or around painted surfaces can sometimes lead to dings and scratches.

The rule of thumb is that when the vehicle was first manufactured on the assembly line, it was built in a controlled environment. Each part was systematically and accurately installed. During the car's lifetime, each and every time parts are removed or replaced, potentially things are compromised. Parts and their hardware (nuts, bolts, clips, threaded parts, etc.) are subjected to bending, cracking, dropping, scratching, puncturing, stripping, and shattering.

This is not to say that cars cannot be maintained and driven for many years and many miles. They can. But new is new, and every car owner must reach a point where he realizes that his vehicle just ain't what it used to be, and never will be.

4. **Grease on the steering wheel or carpet.** Take some precautions yourself and cover your seat and carpets to protect them.

5. **Personal property or change is now missing from the vehicle.** Do not leave *any* valuables in the vehicle.

6. **The repair did not solve the problem.** For example, your car has a hard time starting. The mechanic checks the car and determines that it has not had a tune-up in a long time. (Check the manufacturer's recommended intervals.) He *recommends* one, stating it *might* help. He tunes it up but the car is still hard to start. You're upset because you the consumer just spent $125 or so and are left with the same problem.

From the mechanic's standpoint, it is essential for the engine to have a strong and effective ignition and fuel system, among other things, in order for the car to start and run properly. He must do this basic repair in order to move to the next phase, if necessary. The tune-up may not have solved the difficult starting problem, but it was a needed and necessary step in the repair process. What is important here is that the mechanic communicates to you that the tune-up is necessary, regardless of anything else, and that it may or may not solve the starting problem.

There are many repair scenarios where this type of conflict may arise. Taking the time to communicate and confirm with each other the details of the repair in advance will give both the consumer and the service facility a clear understanding of what is to be expected. Keep in mind that one bad meal at your favorite restaurant does not mean that you should never return. One negative experience at a repair shop does not necessarily constitute that the shop should be blackballed.

Scare Tactics

If the prime motivation of a shop is to make a lot of money by any means necessary, one of those means is to employ scare tactics.

If I did not know better and a "professional" told me that I was on the verge of losing my brakes or losing control of my steering, I would be inclined to fix the problem on the spot.

I think the best way to approach this is to have a "better safe than sorry" attitude. However, you should have your mechanic show you and explain to you exactly why your car needs immediate repair. If he is not convincing, you might want to get a second opinion without delay.

Yes . . . Mechanics Do Screw Up

There is a world of difference between a mechanic who intentionally deceives a customer and one who screws up on a repair job.

Fixing cars is not always easy. Sometimes it seems almost impossible. Errors can be made and situations can develop. These developments can lead to serious consequences. A faulty repair can lead to a car accident or fire, which can result in death or injury. Auto repair is serious business. Hopefully this will never be the case, but the other serious consequences of a faulty repair are expense and inconvenience.

Who should foot the bill for a mechanic's screwup?

People, by nature, have a difficult time accepting responsibility for a mistake. And in the case of your repair facility, a mechanic or his boss might try to cover up an error, especially if it will cost him money or his reputation. If something is broken by accident during a repair, the first inclination of the mechanic is to repair it without even mentioning it to his boss or to the owner of the vehicle. If this repair requires an extensive amount of work or an expensive replacement part, the repair establishment might try to shift the blame on the vehicle or the driver. This could be done by using ploys or terms that are unfamiliar to the owner of the vehicle, or using explanations that would be hard to refute since the customer doesn't understand them.

If you find yourself in this type of situation and you feel uncomfortable or suspicious, do not accept responsibility for it. Instead write down all the details, including the parts that are affected, and tell your shop you will need to get back to them on it. Then do some research. Call other shops and discuss the situation with them and see if they give you the same explanation that your shop has. Look on the Internet or in a repair manual for more information, or you can contact the National Highway Traffic Safety Administration (www.nhtsa.dot.gov) to see if other owners with the same model car have complained about the same problem. Look in the "Defect Investigations" database. If at all possible, ask another mechanic to evaluate the situation for you by coming to see your car and asking the right questions.

Taking control of a situation that is questionable is not always an easy task for a consumer, but it can be done. Consumers can use ploys and tactics also. I think that one of the most powerful tools a consumer can use is his or her mouth. Knowing when to use it is crucial. Winning a one-on-one conversation or argument with a person who knows more than you about your own car is difficult. First of all, arm yourself with as much information as possible, but try not to delve into the technical aspects of it. The mechanic will have the edge over you. Instead, choose a time when his shop is busy with work and with customers. The workload may be enough for them to concede instead of argue, and their concerns for losing other customers that overhear your complaints will be overwhelming. Two popular phrases that most consumers use are, "It was not like that when I left it" and "Ever since you fixed my car." These infer that something was intentionally or accidentally done to their car, resulting in a new problem. These phrases go a long way, and the burden of proof is now on the shop to prove otherwise.

A perfect example of a misconceived screwup happened recently at my shop. First-time customers, husband and wife, complained of a leaking water pump. They said they had been adding water to their radiator for the past three months because of the leak. They also had been adding large doses of motor oil and power steering fluid. After checking over the vehicle, I informed them that in fact they were correct about the leaking water pump and that it needed to be replaced. The power steering fluid was leaking from the rack and pinion and also needed replacement. The motor oil leak, I told them, could only be determined after I washed off the engine and let it run on the lift, because everything under the engine was covered in oil. They authorized the replacement of only the water pump and told me they intended to get rid of the car soon.

I replaced the water pump and filled the system with fresh antifreeze. I allowed the engine to run for thirty minutes, checking to make sure that the coolant was flowing normally and that the electric fans were kicking in properly. I then pressure-tested the cooling system to check for leaks. I topped off the antifreeze and closed the radiator with a new radiator cap. I then let the car run for another fifteen minutes before I released it to the wife.

About a half hour later she called me and informed me that the car had overheated and that she was stuck. I drove to where she was disabled to find that her radiator hose had a small hole in it and her antifreeze had gushed out. I purchased a new hose and replaced it on the spot. I topped off the antifreeze and started the engine. It started right up but it had an engine knock. I slowly drove it back to my shop, where it died. The engine was blown. I called the customers to inform them of the situation. They took the bad news quite well but were certain that the car had overheated because the water pump was defective or installed improperly. They felt, and rightfully so, that the car drove into my shop, but now after the repair, the engine blew.

What happened here? What was the reason the engine overheated after she left? The culprit was the thermostat. It closed and remained shut after she left, preventing the coolant from circulating through the radiator. This caused the engine to overheat. But why did the engine blow so quickly?

In another conversation with the owners they told me a few interesting facts. First, because the water pump had been leaking for three months, the vehicle had overheated a number of times previously. Second, the engine had an oil leak. I was told that when they "heard the engine knocking they knew they had to add oil." This clicked with the fact that I had to add two and a half quarts of oil to the engine when they first brought the car into the shop.

The bottom line: This engine had been subjected to numerous overheats and oil starvations. It was on its last leg before I replaced the water pump, and that last overheating due to the faulty thermostat was the final nail in the coffin.

After I explained this to my customers, they then understood the whole picture. My initial fear was that they thought I was either out for their money or that we had done something wrong that ruined their engine. They were first-time customers and this was no way to start a relationship.

In the end we shook hands and we agreed to split the bill on the water pump. The end.

The Balance Game

For most people, spending money on repair and maintenance is not a pleasant experience by any means. The only way that you as a consumer can look upon the experience positively is if you know the repair was necessary, that the cost was fair, and that

Dilemma

Q: You bring your car in for a repair and your mechanic works on the vehicle, but when all is said and done two hours later, your car is still not repaired. Should you pay the shop for the time spent?

Every situation is different from the next, so this does not have a yes or no answer. What should be considered are the circumstances. If a mechanic uses all of his resources and makes a concerted effort to fix your vehicle but is unable to in the end for reasons beyond his control or abilities, I think that a token of goodwill should be offered—possibly a tip for the mechanic who worked on the car or 25 percent of what the bill would have been if the repair had been successful. This shows your mechanic that you appreciate his efforts even if he did not succeed. If the charge was for diagnostic work that you agreed to up front with a time-limit cap, you should pay as agreed.

the repair was done in a timely fashion. In addition, perks like free pickup and delivery of your vehicle or a loaner car can help to make the experience less painful.

Presenting a customer with a long shopping list of repairs with a hefty bottom line is not exactly the best way to break the ice. Unfortunately for you, it may very well be the case that your car really is in need of these repairs. Your repair facility needs to understand that shocking a customer with a large estimate is risky, but at the same time the consumer has to consider that all the repairs may be necessary. This becomes a delicate balance. Explaining and showing the consumer what a repair is and why it is necessary is the first step. Making a package deal would be step two. Delivering everything you promised to the customer and getting payment would be step three. Having that customer spread the word and refer new customers would be the final step.

This sounds like a beautiful thing, but remember that we are dealing with cars and with people. This mixture can become volatile if the circumstances should change. For instance, if the repair shop legitimately discovers additional work either related or not related to the work already agreed upon, the initial reaction of the customer would be to feel like he is being sucked into a scheme or a scam. This is completely understandable given the reputation that mechanics have for taking advantage of people. However, this scenario has also been part of the cause of this reputation.

For instance: You bring your vehicle in for just an oil change. The technician looks at your brake pads and can see that the linings have worn thin. He suggests that you replace them. He even takes off your front tires and you both get a closer look at your thinned-out brake pads. You give him the okay on the job and tell him you will be back in an hour to pick up your car. The technician starts to replace the brake pads, but when he attempts to press the caliper's piston back into the caliper to allow for the new pads to fit, he discovers that the caliper is tight or seized. The caliper must be replaced to perform the brake job and for the brakes to work properly. The dilemma: He must call you and tell you that the job is going to cost you an additional $140 or so. That is bad news, but it is for a legitimate reason. No scam, no lure. Just a faulty part that the mechanic could not foresee until it was removed to replace the pads. Some customers might be suspicious; some might be convinced they were being scammed. An informed customer like yourself (you are reading this book) will investigate the matter.

The best way to handle this situation is to personally go back to the repair shop and look at this supplement to the initial order. View this repair as an isolated repair and reach your conclusions based on the repair and the circumstances leading up to it. This supplemental repair may have been discovered as a result of closer inspection or by the removal of a cover or part. Consider the fact that everything is on the up and up and remain logical and rational. Always allow your technician to show and explain his point of view and make sure he understands yours.

Attitude

If you develop a chummy rapport or friendship with your repair facility, you end up relying on the merits of that relationship in hopes that the repair shop will be fair and honest with you. You basically waive your rights of being suspicious or insisting on proof that a repair was necessary and completed. After all, it is difficult to be chummy and apprehensive at the same time. Hopefully the repair shop owner or manager will value your friendship and do the right thing.

If you decide to take the approach of keeping it strictly business, having a serious and direct approach with your facility may be beneficial for you if you truly are the serious type or you can pull it off. A serious consumer does not make any small talk. He is there to have his vehicle repaired or maintained. He wants it repaired correctly, the first time, and at the right price. Then he wants to leave. This attitude tells the shop owner that the consumer will not tolerate any "stories" and that he must perform all of his obligations. This type of consumer will not feel awkward in complaining about the cost of a repair or asking to see the replacement parts. This type of consumer will put the shop on alert while making no friends.

Scams

You pull in for gas and the attendant offers to check your oil. He does and says you need a quart. He grabs one from the case and proceeds to pour it into your engine. But what does he pour in? If you were not watching you may have just paid for nothing. The container was empty.

You stop at a service station and the attendant looks under the hood. What you may not see is a sharp razor blade that is used to cut at a belt or a hose. So stay on top of any stranger under your hood.

Your car is on the lift and the technician calls you over to look at your leaking strut or shock absorbers. It looks pretty serious, but it may be because he just squirted oil out of an oil can onto it.

The long and short of it is, you always have to be on the lookout for scams. Following are two of the most popular scams in the business:

Giveaways or low prices for oil changes offer the repair facility an opportunity to look over and under your car. You may legitimately be in need of a repair, but a dishonest mechanic may be luring you onto his lift with the intention of ripping you off.

You pick up your car and pay for the repair. You drive away and never give a second thought as to whether the repair was actually done or the necessary parts have actually been replaced. Before you leave your car for repairs, be curious, ask questions, and look to see what you are being told you need. And ask why.

A mechanic may show you someone else's broken parts when you request to see your replaced parts. If you are suspicious, ask to keep the replaced parts to verify if they came from your car. Ask to see the new parts that were installed on the vehicle. In many cases they are easily visible and noticeably brand-new.

And then there is the superscam: killing two birds with one stone. In this scam the mechanic scams both the consumer and the repair facility.

In large facilities, the mechanic who is assigned to a particular job signs for and picks up from the parts counter the necessary parts to complete the job. He then proceeds to install the parts—but does he? An unscrupulous mechanic may install just some or even none of these parts. Instead he pockets them to be sold on the street or to be installed on a job he takes on the side, perhaps on the weekend.

In highly supervised shops or in small shops where the owner or manager has a "hands on" policy, this scenario is less likely to happen.

Protect yourself and ask to see the old parts. Ask what went wrong with them. Ask to view the new parts that were installed on the vehicle. Many parts are visible at a glance and will be noticeably new and shiny. Make sure you are not looking at parts with a fresh coat of paint. Other parts may be more internal, such as a thermostat or an engine seal. The key is to be curious about the repair from the outset. This will put the repair facility on guard. After all, if you ask a lot of good questions before the repair, chances are you will be inquisitive after the repair.

Emergency Kit

No matter how good a repair is, there is always the chance that your car will break down. Every car should have an emergency kit handy to deal with unexpected problems:

Medical aids: bandages, ace bandage, gauze tape, alcohol swabs, scissors, aspirin, blanket, and high-energy snack bars. (Some new cars come equipped with a first aid kit.)

Automotive: cell phone, battery pack or booster cables, duct tape, electrical tape, length of rope, length of wire, tow rope, air pressure gauge, tire flat fix, compact air compressor, flashlight, extra batteries, road flares, wet wipes, screwdrivers, Vise-Grip, socket set, adjustable wrench, gallon of water, ice scraper and brush (where applicable), umbrella, and a map or atlas.

Reminder: Check your spare tire periodically to make sure it has the correct air pressure.

FAQ: Questions You Have Always Wanted Answered

Q: How does my mechanic make his money?

A: Your mechanic makes his money by periodically maintaining your car, by repairing it (labor) when it breaks down, and on the sale of parts needed for repair.

Q: Should I get a written estimate?

A: You should always get a written estimate, as this will discourage your mechanic from deviating from his original commitment.

Q: Should I ask to see what is actually broken or worn out?

A: Yes! You should see what is broken or worn out, if viewable, both before and after the repairs are made. Your mechanic will then consider you to be an educated and concerned customer. He will also be less likely to try to pull the wool over your eyes.

Q: Should I ask to see, or have, the parts that were replaced?

A: You should ask in advance to see and have, if you have any suspicions, the broken or worn-out parts that were replaced. Some parts, such as starters and alternators, are generally rebuilt and the replaced part must be returned to the rebuilder to avoid paying a core charge. You can ask to see them before they are returned.

Q: Should I ask to see how long the labor guide allows for a particular repair?

A: You should ask to see the labor guidebook, which indicates how many hours the repair should take the mechanic so labor costs can be determined according to his hourly labor rate.

Q: Should I compare prices?

A: You should call other repair shops in advance to compare prices or the dealership to see what they charge. You should find out what their labor rate per hour is and compare it to other shops in the area.

Q: Should I try to negotiate a better deal?

A: Everything is negotiable. If you feel your estimate is too high or you are just trying to save money, make an offer. Nobody wants to see a job drive away, and some shops would prefer to make less money on a job than no money at all. The best time to negotiate a deal is when your shop is slow.

Q: Should I ask for a written guarantee?

A: You should ask for a written guarantee on both the parts and the labor.

Q: How should I pay for the repair?

A: Payment by credit card affords you the advantage to dispute payment. When you pay in cash you will need to take legal steps in the event of a dispute.

Q: How should I choose my repair shop?

A: Choosing your repair shop is very important. Select it the same way you would select a doctor. We are discussing the health and well-being of your car, which affects your safety and the safety of others. The best way to choose one is to use other people's previous experiences with their shops. If they are satisfied over a period of time, then chances are you will be also.

Let specialists like transmission shops repair transmissions, muffler shops repair exhausts, diagnostic and electrical shops repair shorts, body shops repair dents, and tire shops repair tires and alignments. They will more likely be proficient in these specific repairs than a general service station.

Q: Should I test-drive the car before paying?

A: You should test-drive your car (if applicable) before paying, if possible, to ensure satisfaction.

Q: If I am not satisfied with the repair, what should I do?

A: If you are not satisfied with the repair, always give the mechanic a chance to remedy the complaint. If the mechanic is a good businessman he will want to keep you happy. He knows that:

> *A happy customer is a repeat customer.*

> *A happy customer is a good source of advertising.*

Be patient and direct. The last thing a shop wants is a loud unsatisfied customer in their crowded waiting room. If all else fails, you can turn to the courts, the Department of Motor Vehicles, the Department of Consumer Affairs, and the Better Business Bureau.

Q: Should I give the mechanic or manager a copy of my "to do" list so they do not miss anything?

A: Definitely. There is nothing more frustrating than to have to leave your car for an extra day because of an oversight.

Q: Should I tip the mechanic?

A: Yes. Even a small gesture of appreciation can go a long way. Some mechanics will remember this the next time you come in for a repair.

Q: How can I keep my repair cost from becoming inflated?

A: Some jobs are not straightforward with a preestablished cost. Some repairs require time to diagnose or troubleshoot. Because of this it would be hard for your mechanic to give you a set price in advance of the diagnosis.

What you can do in advance is to try to have your mechanic agree to a worst-case scenario with a bottom line or have him stop the clock if he has not found the problem after two hours of searching.

The bottom line is that you want to find yourself in the hands of a mechanic whom you have been satisfied with over a period of time. The confidence he has earned over time will reassure you he is trying to diagnose your problem efficiently and effectively.

Q: How do I spot a liar?

A: Do what detectives do—question the suspects separately. Before you leave your car, ask which mechanic will be working on your vehicle. When you return to pick it up, mosey over to that mechanic and ask him how things went. Ask him what he did, what was replaced, and if there were any problems. Also ask him how long the repair took. Then ask the bossman the same questions in private and see if there are any discrepancies.

"Wait and watch"—find a facility that will not mind if you get involved to some extent with the repair. This does not mean that you help do the actual repair but that you are able to ask questions and are able to "wait and watch." It is much harder to pull the wool over someone's eyes when they are aware and watching. You can also keep track of the amount of time the mechanic is actually working on your car.

Mechanics have been stigmatized as being dishonest and taking advantage of customers by overcharging, performing shabby repairs, not repairing what they billed for, selling unnecessary repairs, and even damaging something to create business. It is not a pretty picture, but as in all professions, the auto repair industry is so vast that mechanics range from very honest and ethical to very dishonest and unethical.

Where will you end up?

Glossary of Terms

ABS (antilock braking system)
a system that senses when a wheel has stopped spinning during braking. It rapidly releases brake pressure, causing the wheel to spin as slowly as possible without locking up and skidding. This is especially effective in rain and snow.

air filter
a disposable device that catches small airborne particles before they enter the engine's intake

alignment
the proper adjustment of the angles of the wheels in relation to the vehicle and one another

axle
a rotating shaft that rotates another part, such as a wheel

backfire
when the fuel ignites in the engine at an improper time, causing a loud explosion

ball joint
a component of the front suspension that allows the wheels to pivot during steering while at the same time going up and down over bumps

band
in an automatic transmission, a device used to prevent members of a planetary gearset from rotating

battery
a device that produces and stores electricity through electrochemical action

battery acid   the sulfuric acid solution used as the electrolyte in a battery

bead   the steel-reinforced inner edge of a tire, which fits inside and seals against the wheel rim

bearing   a part that supports and reduces friction between a stationary and moving part or two moving parts

bearing clearance   the space between a bearing and its corresponding component's loaded surface. Bearing clearances are commonly provided to allow lubrication between the parts.

bearing race   the machined surface of a bearing assembly against which the needles, balls, or rollers ride. The outer race is also called a cup.

before top dead center (BTDC)   the degree of crankshaft rotation just before the piston in a specific cylinder reaches TDC, the highest point in its vertical travel on the compression stroke. On most vehicles, spark occurs at a certain number of degrees of crankshaft rotation BTDC.

bell housing   connects the engine to the transmission and encloses the clutch assembly. It also provides mounting points for part of the clutch release mechanism.

bias   diagonal line of direction. In reference to tires, bias means that belts and plies are laid diagonally or crisscross each other.

bleeder valve   a valve located on disc brake calipers, wheel cylinders, and some master cylinders that allows air and fluid to be removed from the brake system. Some cooling systems also have bleeder valves to allow for air to escape from the cooling system.

blowby
the unburned fuel and products of combustion that are forced past the piston rings and into the crankcase during the combustion stroke

blower motor
the electric motor that drives the fan that circulates air inside a vehicle's passenger compartment

boot
a protective rubber cover with accordion pleats used to contain lubricants and exclude contaminating dirt, water, and grime, located at each end of the rack-and-pinion assembly and CV joints

brake drag
a condition that occurs when brake pads or shoes are in continuous contact with the disc brake rotors or brake drums

brake drum
a round cast-iron housing attached to an axle shaft or spindle on which the brake shoes press to stop its rotation

brake fade
a phenomenon that occurs when the temperature of the friction surfaces increases to a point where the application of heavy pedal pressure results in little braking action

brake fluid
the hydraulic fluid used to transmit hydraulic pressure through the brake lines in a brake system

brake flushing
a procedure to clean the brake hydraulic system with fresh, clean fluid that should be performed whenever new parts are installed or if the fluid is contaminated

brake hoses
flexible hoses that connect the brake lines on the chassis with the calipers or wheel cylinders, or the junction block on a solid axle

brake lines
metal tubing that carries the brake fluid from the master cylinder to other brake system components

brake shoes — friction material that is bonded or riveted to curved metal structures and attached to the backing plate. The brake shoes press on the brake drum to stop its rotation.

break-in — a slow wearing-in process between two mating part surfaces

bushing — a component of the suspension system, usually made from rubber (rubber and metal), that provides a cushion between moving parts

camber — the attitude of a wheel/tire assembly in which, when viewed from the front or rear of the vehicle, the distance between the tops and bottoms of two tires is different. If the distance between the tops is greater than between the bottoms, positive camber is present. If the distance between the tops is less than between the bottoms, negative camber is present.

camshaft — a shaft with eccentric lobes that control the opening of the intake and exhaust valves

camshaft sprocket — the sprocket on a camshaft that is turned by a chain or belt from the crankshaft. The camshaft sprocket has twice as many teeth as the crankshaft sprocket.

carbon monoxide (CO) — a colorless, odorless gas that is highly poisonous. CO is produced by incomplete combustion. It is absorbed by the bloodstream 400 times faster than oxygen.

carburetor — a device that atomizes air and fuel in a proportion that is burnable in the engine

caster — the angle formed between the kingpin axis and a vertical axis as viewed from the side of the vehicle. Caster is considered positive when the top of the kingpin axis is behind the vertical axis, that is, tilted toward the rear of the vehicle.

catalyst

a compound or substance that can speed up or slow down the reaction of other substances without being consumed itself. In a catalytic converter, special metals (platinum or palladium) are used to promote combustion of unburned hydrocarbons and reduce carbon monoxide emissions.

catalytic converter

an emission control device located in the exhaust system that contains catalysts that reduce hydrocarbons, carbon monoxide, and nitrogen oxides in the exhaust gases

centerlink

a steering linkage component that attaches the pitman arm to the idler arm, tie rod, or crosslink

centrifugal force

the force that pulls an object outward when it is rotating rapidly around a center axis

charging system

the system that supplies electrical power for vehicle operation and recharges the battery

check engine light, or malfunction indicator light (MIL)

a light on a car's instrument panel that illuminates when the onboard computer determines a diagnostic trouble code

clutch

in a manual transmission, a device that allows the driver to engage and disengage the engine from the drivetrain; in an automatic transmission, a device capable of both holding and turning members of a planetary gearset; a device used to engage and disengage the A/C compressor

clutch pressure plate

the part of the clutch assembly that holds the driving disc against the flywheel. The pressure plate is composed of a cover and coil springs, driving disc and release levers, or a diaphragm spring.

clutch release bearing

a sealed ball or roller bearing unit that rides on a sleeve over the transmission input shaft and acts on the pressure plate to disengage the clutch disc when the clutch release mechanism is applied. Also called the throwout bearing.

coil spring

a spring steel rod wound into a coil that supports the vehicle's weight while allowing suspension movement

cold cranking amps

the amount of cranking amperes that a battery can deliver in thirty seconds at zero degrees Fahrenheit (minus 18 degrees Celsius)

compressor

an engine-driven device that compresses refrigerant gas and pumps it through the air-conditioning system

condenser

a device, similar to a radiator, in which the refrigerant loses heat and changes state from a high-pressure gas to a high-pressure liquid as it dissipates heat into the surrounding air

connecting rod

a rod that connects the crankshaft to the piston and enables the reciprocating motion of the piston to turn the crankshaft

constant velocity (CV) joint

a device attached to both ends of an axle enabling it to spin and pivot at the same time

coolant

the mixture of water and antifreeze used in an engine's cooling system to maintain the engine's temperature throughout its operating range

cooling system

the system used to remove excess heat from an engine and transfer it to the atmosphere. Includes the radiator, cooling fan, hoses, water pump, thermostat, and engine coolant passages

crankshaft
a lower engine part with main and rod bearing surfaces. It converts reciprocating motion to rotary motion.

cylinder head
the casting that contains the valves and valve springs and covers the top of the cylinders

detonation
abnormal combustion of an air/fuel mixture, when pressure in the cylinder becomes excessive and the mixture explodes violently, instead of burning in a controlled manner. The sound of detonation can be heard as the cylinder walls vibrate. Detonation is sometimes confused with preignition or ping.

dial indicator
a measuring device equipped with a readout dial, used most often to determine end motion or irregularities

dipstick
a thin metal blade that is used to measure the level of oil or transmission fluid. Motor oil is measured with the engine off, while transmission fluid is measured with the engine running and the transmission in park. Both dipstick measurements should be taken with the vehicle on level ground.

direct ignition
a distributorless ignition system in which spark distribution is controlled by a computer

directional tires
tires with a tread pattern that is designed to give maximum traction by removing water from under the tread in such a way as to minimize the risk of aquaplaning. Directional tires must be installed to spin in a specific direction.

disc brake
a braking system that uses iron discs mounted on the wheel hubs, over which

brake calipers are mounted. Hydraulic pressure from the brake system forces the caliper piston(s) against friction pads mounted in the calipers, which in turn clamp the brake discs, stopping their rotation.

disc brake caliper   a hydraulically actuated device in a disc brake system that is mounted straddling the brake disc. The caliper contains at least one piston and is used to provide clamping force of the brake pads on the disc.

disc brake pads   friction material that is bonded or riveted to metal plates and mounted in the disc brake caliper. The brake pads clamp against the disc brake rotor to stop its rotation.

disc brake rotor   a cast-iron disc mounted on the wheel hub, which is clamped by the caliper and disc brake pads to slow and stop its rotation

distributor cap   a device that sits on top of the engine's distributor and provides an electrical connection between the ignition coil and each specific spark plug

drivability   the degree to which a vehicle operates properly, including starting, running smoothly, accelerating, and delivering reasonable fuel mileage

driveline   all of the parts connecting the engine to the drive axles

drivetrain   all of the components that generate power and transfer it to the vehicle's wheels

drum brake   a braking system that uses cast-iron drums mounted to the wheel hubs. Hydraulic pressure from the brake system forces pistons in the wheel cylinder to press friction-lined brake shoes against the inside of the drum, stopping its rotation.

DTC (diagnostic trouble code)
: a code that is retrieved from the onboard computer by a scanner when troubleshooting a check engine light

dual master cylinder
: a master cylinder that has one cylinder bore, but two pistons and two fluid reservoirs. Each piston applies hydraulic pressure to two wheels only. In the event that one of the hydraulic circuits fails, the other provides enough braking power to stop the vehicle.

electronic control module (ECM)
: the computer in an electronic control system; also known as an electronic control unit (ECU)

evaporator
: a heat exchanger in which low-pressure refrigerant flows and changes state, absorbing heat from the surrounding air

exhaust manifold
: the first stage of the exhaust system, where the exhaust leaves the engine

expansion tube
: used in some air-conditioning systems; a component with a fixed opening through which refrigerant passes as it is metered into the evaporator core. Also called an orifice tube.

expansion valve
: used on some air-conditioning systems; a temperature-sensitive device that meters flow of refrigerant into the evaporator core. Also called a thermostatic expansion valve (TXV).

final drive
: on front-wheel-drive vehicles, the central connecting point of the front axles

flooding
: a condition in which unvaporized fuel in the intake manifold and/or combustion area prevents the engine from starting

flywheel
: a cast-iron or steel wheel mounted to the end of the crankshaft; helps to smooth the engine's power delivery, the teeth around its circumference provide an engagement for the

front-wheel drive   starter, and it provides the mounting points for the pressure plate and friction surface for the clutch disc and for the torque converter (on automatic transmissions)

front-wheel drive   a system in which the entire drivetrain is located at the front of and drives the front wheels of the vehicle

fuel filter   a disposable device that catches small particles in the fuel before they enter the engine fuel intake

fuel injector   an electrically opened nozzle that sprays finely atomized fuel through its aperture into the intake manifold during a cylinder's intake stroke. On some vehicles these injections are sequential; on others the injectors are fired all at once or in banks.

fuse   a replaceable link that protects an electrical circuit from overload by burning out and opening a circuit

gasket   a material such as artificial rubber, cork, or steel used to seal between parts that would otherwise leak fuel, coolant, lubricants, or combustion gases

hangers   rubber devices from which the exhaust system is suspended

heater core   a radiator-like device used to heat the inside of a vehicle. Hot coolant is pumped through it by the water pump, and heat from the coolant moves from the heater core to the passenger compartment as the blower fan forces air through it.

high side   the high-pressure half of an A/C system; usually refers to all components between the compressor outlet and the expansion valve or expansion tube. In this part of the A/C system, the refrigerant is in a liquid form.

horsepower (HP)   a measurement of an engine's ability to perform work. One horsepower is the energy required to lift 550 pounds one foot in one second.

hub   the mounting point for the wheel on an axle or spindle; the part of the synchronizer assembly that is splined to the transmission shaft; the center part of a wheel, gear, etc., that rides on a shaft

hydraulic valve lifter   an automatic lash adjusting device that provides a rigid connection between the camshaft and valve, while absorbing the shock of motion. A hydraulic valve lifter differs from the solid type in that it uses oil to absorb the shock that results from movement of the valvetrain.

hydro-boost   a power brake system that uses power steering pump fluid pressure rather than an intake manifold vacuum

idler arm   a conventional steering system component consisting of an arm that swivels in a bushing on a shaft, which is attached to the frame. The idler arm is mounted on the right side of the vehicle and is the same length and set at the same angle as the pitman arm. Its function is to hold the right end of the centerlink level with the left end, which is moved by the pitman arm, and transfer the steering motion to the right-side tie rod.

ignition coil   transforms the low, 12-volt battery ignition primary current into the high-voltage secondary current that fires the spark in the spark plugs. The current through the primary coil windings builds up an electromagnetic field around the ferrous core of the coil. When the current is suddenly shut off, the electromagnetic field collapses and generates the high voltage in the secondary windings.

ignition control module (ICM)

the computer does not directly operate the ignition coil because of the comparatively high voltages and current involved. Instead, it signals the ignition control module when to fire the spark. The ICM has a power transistor that turns on the ignition primary circuit to charge the coil by building an electromagnetic field around the ferrous core, and fires the spark by shutting off the current to the primary circuit, allowing the field to collapse and generate a high-voltage spark current in the coil secondary circuit. The ignition control module typically includes additional internal circuits to perform other functions, such as calculating dwell. Some modern systems have dwell and timing control in the PCM, relegating the ICM to the duties of an on/off switch for the coil.

ignition system

the components that produce the spark to ignite the air/fuel mixture in the combustion chamber

ignition timing

refers in crankshaft degrees to the position of the piston in the cylinder when the spark occurs

ignition wires

the wires that carry electric current from the engine's distributor to the spark plugs

independent suspension

a suspension in which each wheel can travel up and down without directly affecting the position of the opposite wheel

low side — the suction side of an A/C system between the evaporator core inlet (after the expansion valve or expansion tube) and the compressor. In this part of the A/C system, the refrigerant is in a gas form.

MacPherson strut — the principal device in the suspension of the same name, in which the spring, shock absorber, and sometimes the steering knuckle are combined in a single unit

malfunction indicator light (MIL) — also known as the check engine or service engine soon light on many vehicles. The MIL comes on when the ignition is first turned on (to check the bulb) and then goes out once the engine is started, unless a trouble code is stored in the computer. If the MIL comes on when the vehicle is running, there has been a malfunction on one of the sensor or actuator circuits monitored by the computer, and a diagnosis will have to be made by retrieving the code.

master cylinder — the primary fluid pressurizing device in some hydraulic systems. In automotive use, it is found in the brake and hydraulic clutch systems and is pedal-activated, either directly or through a vacuum-assist unit.

misfire — failure of an explosion to occur in one or more cylinders while the engine is running; can be continuous or intermittent failure

muffler — a component of the exhaust system that deadens the sound created by the fuel burning in the engine's combustion chamber

multiviscosity — having the properties of more than one viscosity level. Oil can be chemically modified to expand its viscosity range, allowing it to react in a similar fashion at various temperatures.

neutral start (safety) switch a switch that prevents starter engagement if the transmission is in another gear besides park or neutral

OBD-II the onboard diagnostic computer system (second generation) that detects the deterioration of emission controls or powertrain components and actively adjusts components to maximize performance and efficiency. OBD-II has been a federally mandated system since 1996; it monitors emission control systems for degradation as well as for failure.

octane a rating indicating a fuel's tendency to resist detonation

oil pan the part that encloses the crankcase at the lower end of the engine block

oil pressure the pressure that results from resistance to flow from the oil pump. As the pump turns faster, it produces more flow. A relief valve limits the amount of pressure it can produce.

oil pump the pump that circulates lubricating oil throughout the engine, usually driven by the camshaft (by way of the distributor)

onboard diagnostic (OBD) a diagnostic software system in the ECM or PCM (powertrain control module) that monitors computer inputs, outputs, and resultant engine/transmission operations for failure. OBD-I is thought of as any of the systems in use before OBD-II, typically from 1979 to 1995, although some manufacturers started transitioning to OBD-II in 1994 and 1995.

oxygen sensor a sensor that consists of a ceramic zirconium thimble, coated on each side with a very thin film of platinum. Once it reaches operating temperature of 600 degrees Fahrenheit, the oxygen sensor begins to function as a very low-current battery, producing between zero and one volt with the output corresponding to the difference in oxygen level between the exhaust and the ambient air. The signal from the oxygen sensor enables the computer to keep the air/fuel mixture as close as possible to the stoichiometric (chemically correct) mixture of 14.7 parts air to one part fuel. Under normal conditions, the oxygen sensor signal should fluctuate above and below 450 millivolts several times a second while the system is in closed loop.

parking brake　a system that applies the brakes mechanically through a series of linkages and cables. Depending on the vehicle, the parking brake system will either be actuated using a foot pedal or a hand-operated lever.

PCV valve　a part of the positive crankcase ventilation system; meters crankcase vapors into the intake manifold

pilot bearing　a needle roller bearing, installed in the end of the crankshaft, that supports the end of the transmission input shaft

piston　the cylindrical component that is attached to the connecting rod and moves up and down in the cylinder bore. The top of the piston forms the bottom of the combustion chamber. When combustion occurs, the piston is forced downward in the cylinder, moving the connecting rod, which in turn rotates the crankshaft.

pitman arm　a steering system component mounted on the steering box shaft that transfers the gearbox motion to the steering linkage

power booster   a device that uses a diaphragm, engine vacuum, and atmospheric pressure to assist the driver with brake application; also known as a vacuum booster

proportioning valve   a valve used to control hydraulic pressure to the rear brakes. When the pressure to the rear brakes reaches a predetermined level, the proportioning valve overcomes the force of its spring-loaded piston and stops the flow of fluid to the rear brakes. This action maintains rear brake system pressure at a lower level than the front brakes, keeping the rear brakes from locking during hard stops.

pull   a steering condition in which the vehicle's driver has to maintain constant pressure on the steering wheel to keep the vehicle moving straight

R12   the generic term for the CFC refrigerant used in older A/C systems

R134a   a generic term for a modern refrigerant that does not contain CFCs and does not harm the ozone layer

race   a channel in the inner or outer ring of an antifriction bearing in which the balls or rollers operate

rack-and-pinion steering   a type of steering mechanism that replaces the pitman arm, center link, and idler arm on gearbox steering. The steering column ends in a pinion gear that moves the driven rack to the left and right. The rack ends contain ball studs connected to the outer tie rods and steering knuckles.

radiator   the part of the cooling system that acts as a heat exchanger, transferring heat to the atmosphere. It consists of a core and holding tanks connected to the cooling system by hoses.

rear main oil seal   a seal that fits around the rear of the crankshaft to prevent oil leaks

rear-wheel drive   a system in which the driveline drives the rear wheels of the vehicle. Most often the engine is located in the front of the vehicle and a transmission and driveshaft connect to a drive axle; however, there are also systems where the entire driveline is located toward the rear of the vehicle.

relay   an electromagnetic switch that uses low-amperage current to control a circuit with high amperage

revving (revolutions)   a term used to describe the spinning of an engine

resonator   an auxiliary component of the exhaust system that deadens sound created by the fuel burning in the engine's combustion chamber

rpm   revolutions per minute

scalloping   a tire pattern, caused by wheel imbalance, in which pieces appear to be cut out of the tire by a spoon

scan tool   a microprocessor designed to communicate with a vehicle's onboard computer system to perform diagnostic and troubleshooting functions

seize   when a part sticks, preventing the engine from turning. An example is when a piston welds itself to a cylinder wall because of insufficient clearance, lubrication, or excessive heat.

sensor   any mechanism by which the engine control computer can measure some variable on the engine, such as coolant temperature or engine speed. Each sensor works by sending the computer a signal of some sort, a coded electronic message that corresponds to some point on the range of the variable measured by that sensor.

serpentine belt   a flat, ribbed drive belt that makes multiple angles, driving several components

shock absorber   a device used to dampen the oscillation of the suspension caused by irregularities in the road surface

sight glass   a window in the high-pressure side of the A/C system, usually in the receiver-drier, for observing the refrigerant for signs of bubbles and/or moisture

slave cylinder   a device that is connected to the release bearing in a hydraulic clutch system. When the clutch pedal is depressed, hydraulic fluid flows from the master cylinder through the hydraulic fluid line to the slave cylinder. Pressure in the system causes the slave cylinder to act on the release bearing, disengaging the clutch.

solenoid   a device that reacts to electrical current, causing a mechanical movement

spark plug   a disposable device that screws into the head of an engine and delivers the electrical spark needed to ignite the air/fuel mixture in the combustion chamber

spindle   a shaft used to attach the wheel assembly on non-drive axles

spring   a suspension system component that supports the vehicle and absorbs shock caused by uneven road surfaces

steering box (gear)	an assembly located at the end of the steering column that contains the gears and other components that multiply turning force exerted on the steering wheel
struts (MacPherson struts)	the principal device in the suspension of the same name in which the spring, shock absorber, and sometimes the steering knuckle are combined in a single unit
synchronizer	a type of clutch assembly used in a manual transmission in order to shift gears without grinding
tailpipe	a component of the exhaust system that transfers the exhaust out of the rear of the vehicle
tapered ends	the end of the lug nut that narrows down to allow the rim to be centered on the hub
technical service bulletin (TSB)	information published by a vehicle manufacturer that describes updated service procedures that should be used to handle vehicle defects
thermostat	a device installed in the cooling system that allows the engine to come to operating temperature quickly and then maintain a minimum operating temperature
throttle body injection (TBI)	also called central fuel injection; it has an intake manifold that is used with a carburetor. One or more fuel injectors are mounted in the throttle body, which resembles a carburetor in physical appearance.
tie rod	a steering linkage member that connects the steering knuckle arm with the centerlink or the steering rack
timing belt	a toothed reinforced belt used to drive the camshaft from a sprocket on the crankshaft

timing chain   a chain that drives the camshaft from a sprocket on the crankshaft

tire rotation   the practice of moving a set of tires to different positions on the vehicle to equalize wear and extend the life of the tires

toe-in   a condition that exists when the tire's line of forward direction intersects the extended centerline of the vehicle

toe-out   a condition that exists if the tire's line of forward direction and the vehicle centerline are angled apart

torque   a specific amount of pressure, measured in foot-pounds or inches, in tightening some bolts and nuts

torque converter   a component of the automatic transmission that uses hydraulic fluid to engage the engine to the transmission

transmission   a system that transfers the engine's power to the driveshaft and the rear wheels. Contains a series of gears that provide torque multiplication, so the vehicle can be moved from a standstill and also cruise at highway speeds at lower engine rpm.

universal joint (U-joint)   a joint that allows the driveshaft to transmit torque at different angles as the suspension moves up and down

valvetrain   a system that converts camshaft movement to valve movement. Includes the camshaft, cam timing parts, lifters or cam followers, pushrods, rocker arms, valve, and spring.

viscosity   the ability to lubricate

water pump   a device used to circulate water through the cooling system

wheel alignment	the adjustment of suspension and steering components to optimize steering control and minimize tire wear
wheel balance	the condition in which a wheel/tire assembly has equal weight distribution around its center, preventing vibration at high speeds. Wheel balance can be static, such as on a bubble balancer, or dynamic, such as with a spin balancer.
wheel cylinder	a cylinder connected to a drum brake hydraulic system. Hydraulic pressure in the system applies piston(s) in the wheel cylinder against the brake shoes, forcing the shoes against the inside of the brake drum and stopping its rotation.
wheel speed sensor	a permanent magnetic sensor that sends information regarding wheel speed to the computer in an ABS system

Index

About the Author

Born and raised in Brooklyn, New York, MITCHELL ZELMAN attended Yeshiva of Flatbush, Midwood High School, and Brooklyn College. His interest in cars was sparked by his older brother of nine years, who was indoctrinated into the hot rod–muscle car scene even before he could legally drive. As a child Mitchell built model cars, worked on bicycles and lawn mower engines, and then subsequently built motorized bicycles. He enjoyed fixing things that were broken, and at the age of fifteen purchased his first car, a 1969 Plymouth Barracuda. This car offered him the opportunity to learn about and to repair cars, as it was in constant need of repairs. Mitchell developed skills in auto repair and further enhanced them by working for master mechanics at various repair shops. In his twenties he opened and operated a gas and inspection station/repair shop and went on to design aerodynamic kits for sports cars. He has been in the auto repair business for twenty-seven years and currently owns and operates Mitchell's Auto Repair in Brooklyn.